ISBN 978-1-330-93189-9
PIBN 10123004

Similar Books Are Available from
www.forgottenbooks.com

PUNCH AND JUDY,

WITH TWENTY-FOUR ILLUSTRATIONS.

DESIGNED AND ENGRAVED BY

GEORGE CRUIKSHANK.

AND OTHER PLATES.

ACCOMPANIED BY THE DIALOGUE OF THE PUPPET-SHOW,
AN ACCOUNT OF ITS ORIGIN, AND OF PUPPET PLAYS
IN ENGLAND.

FIFTH EDITION.

LONDON:
BELL & DALDY, YORK STREET, COVENT GARDEN.
1870.

LONDON:
PRINTED BY WILLIAM CLOWES AND SONS,
STAMFORD STREET AND CHARING CROSS.

EXTRACT FROM THE CATALOGUE OF THE CRUIKSHANK EXHIBITION.

"HAVING been engaged by Mr. PROWETT, the publisher, to give the various scenes represented in the street performances of 'Punch and Judy,' I obtained the address of the Proprietor and Performer of that popular Exhibition. He was an elderly Italian, of the name of PICCINI, whom I remembered from boyhood, and he lived at a low public-house, the sign of 'The King's Arms,' in the 'Coal-yard,' 'Drury Lane.' Having made arrangements for a 'Morning Performance,' one of the window-frames on the first floor of the public-house was taken out, and the stand or Punch's Theatre was hauled into the 'Club-room.' Mr. PAYNE COLLIER (who was to write the description), the publisher, and myself, formed the audience; and as the performance went on, I stopped it at the most interesting parts to sketch the Figures, whilst Mr. COLLIER noted down the dialogue; and thus the whole is a faithful copy and description of the various scenes represented by this Italian, whose performance of 'Punch' was far superior in every respect to anything of the sort to be seen at the present day. The figure whose neck he used to stretch to such a great height, was a sort of interlude. PICCINI made the figure take off his hat with one hand—which he defied all other puppet-show performers to do. PICCINI announced the approach of Punch by sound of trumpet.

GEORGE CRUIKSHANK."

3

CONTENTS.

LIST OF GEORGE CRUIKSHANK'S PICTURES OF PUNCH.

OTHER ILLUSTRATIONS NOT BY MR. GEORGE CRUIKSHANK.

INTRODUCTION.

WITH the assistance of our friend, Mr. GEORGE CRUIKSHANK, we are about to fill up a *hiatus* in theatrical history.

It is singular, that, to the present day, no attempt has been made to illustrate the origin, biography, and character of a person so distinguished and notorious as Mr. PUNCH. His name and his performances are familiar to all ranks and ages; yet nobody has hitherto taken the trouble, in this country or abroad, to make any enquiries regarding himself, his family, or connections. The "studious Bayle" is recorded to have repeatedly sallied from his retreat, at the sound of the cracked trumpet, announcing his arrival in Rotterdam; and we ourselves, who have often hunted our favourite performer from street to street, saw the late Mr. Windham, then one of the Secretaries of State, on his way from Downing Street to the House of Commons, on a night of important debate, pause like a truant boy, until the whole performance was concluded, to enjoy a hearty laugh at the whimsicalities of " the motley hero." But it is needless to particularise.—Punch has

" made our youth to laugh,
" Until they scarcely could look out for tears;"

while the old have stood by, " delighted with delight" of others, and themselves, too, enjoying the ludicrous representation. Why the interest has hitherto been limited to the period of representation, and whether it has not in part arisen from inability to satisfy it, is not for us to explain. We confine ourselves to an endeavour in some degree, to supply the deficiency.

The contrast between the neglect **Mr.** Punch has experienced, and the industry employed in collecting particulars relating to other performers of far less reputation, is remarkable. If an actor, on any of our public stages, attain only a moderate degree of eminence, hundreds are on the alert to glean the minutest particulars of his " birth, parentage, and education, life, character, and behaviour;" and thousands look out for them with eagerness in all the newspapers and periodicals of the day. Punch has never been *famæ petitor:*

    " That last distemper of the sober brain,"*

---

    * How this unhappy thought has run the gauntlet of authorship from the time of Simplicius (Comm. ad Epict. xlviii.) Δίο χαι εσχατος, λεγετχι των παδων, &c. Tacitus has it thus; "Etiam sapientibus cupido gloriæ novissima exuitur." (Hist. Lib. iv.) Montaigne places the love of glory among the *humeurs desraisonnables* of men, and adds, " Les philosophes mêmes se defacent plus tard, et plus envis, de cette-cy que de nulle autre." (*Essays,* L. i. c. 41.) Ben Jonson says the same thing :

    " Ambition—is the last affection
        A high mind can put off."—(*Catiline,* Act 3, Sc. 2.)

It is also found in Massinger ·

    " Though desire of fame be the last weakness
        Wise men put off.—(*A Very Woman,* Act 5, Sc. 4.)

And Owen Feltham follows Tacitus very closely : " Desire of glory is the last garment that even wise men lay aside." — (*Resolves,* p. 15.)

as Marvell calls it, has never been one of his weaknesses; but, nevertheless, it is undeniable, that his fame has spread, " without his stirring," over all the kingdoms of the civilized world. To use the wordy periphrasis of Dr. Johnson,

> " Let observation, with extensive view
> " Survey mankind from China to Peru ;"

if it can, and it will everywhere behold Punch dispensing " the luxury of a laugh." It is literally true, that, some years ago, he found his way to Canton; and that, since the South American Revolution he has been seen even on the western side of the Andes. He is, perhaps, himself in part to blame for the neglect we have noticed. Several of the principal supporters of our theatres, in our own day, have given their memoirs to the world, either by writing them with their own hands, or by furnishing the materials to others; and the works of this kind by dead actors, " the forgotten of the stage," consist of many volumes. Whether it has arisen from an absence of that vanity (may we call it?) which has at times influenced his histrionic rivals, or from a somewhat haughty reluctance, on his part, to gratify public curiosity, we know not; but whatever injury it may do the sale of our volume, 'it

---

We may wind up the whole with Milton, who, like others, has deemed the thought common property, when he tells us in *Lycidas*, that fame is
> " That last infirmity of noble mind :"

upon which, in fact, Marvel's line, above quoted (and which is to be found in his "Satire on Flecno, an English priest, at Rome") is only a parody.

ought not in fairness to be concealed, that, towards us, the object and subject of the appended inquiry has preserved an obstinate silence which, in any other individual, we should say amounted to incivility. Even when informed that his portrait was to be drawn by Mr. George Cruikshank, it did not at all change his deportment. This circumstance is certainly to be regretted; but we flatter ourselves that our unaided resources have furnished much curious and interesting information : and if, by its publication, we give offence, we must "aby the event," knowing that, as Mr. Punch was deaf to our request, he will not listen to our apology.

Another remark may not here be out of its place: Poetry is unquestionably out of fashion; and because it was not " set by," as perhaps it ought to have been, the greatest (in every sense of the word) author of the day turned his attention to a different and more popular mode of writing. His astonishing success induced others to follow his example: they, too, tried their hands at historical novels; but, wanting the genius of their original, they endeavoured to keep up the interest of their narratives by the introduction of biographical matter. Still they found they were not read, and their next step was to make the dead the means of satirising and censuring the living; until, in a short time, this thin disguise was thrown aside, and novels became the vehicles of private anecdotes and malicious disclosures. Such is now the characteristic of our literature, excepting in as far as it was corrected by the "Colossus" aforesaid; and we appeal to all the puffs in all the papers for the proof, that fashionable slander, and the exposure of secret intrigues of persons in high life have been made the chief recommendation and attraction of such productions. The course has been, to assign the work of a " scribbling garreteer" to some lord or lady of distinguished connections, and to represent, that, for the sake of gratifying a mania for the consumption of pen, ink, and paper, he or she has condescended, first to play the spy, and afterwards the traitor, to friends and acquaintances.

Nothing of this kind will be found in the volume now in the reader's hand ; and although the biography of the Punch family is, necessarily, partially included in our plan, those who expect that we shall detail particulars of his private amours and failings will be disappointed. Ariosto tells such as may not like certain parts of his gay poem, to turn over so many of its leaves :* we advise those, who feel vexation at the preceding statement, to shut our book altogether ; or, at least, not to do more than cast their eyes upon the plates : since they know by whom the drawings were made, it would, perhaps, be too much to suppose they could consent to relinquish that gratification. Those incidents of his life which our hero has chosen to make known, are of course not omitted ; but, in our details and observations, we have spoken of him only in his public capacity,—as an actor of first-rate talents and the most extensive celebrity.

---

* See the introductory stanzas to Book xxviii. of the "Orlando Furioso."

" Lasciate questo canto, che senz' esso,
Può star l'istoria," &c.

ILLUSTRATIONS OF THE COSTUMES OF ITALIAN COMEDY,

From Riccoboni.

HARLEQUIN.   PANTALOON.   DOCTOR.   PUNCH.
(*Ancient.*)   (*Ancient.*)   (*Modern.*)   (*Neapolitan.*)

SCAPIN.   MEZZETIN.   PIERROT.   SCARAMOUCHE.
(*Neapolitan.*)

CHAPTER I.

MR. PUNCH (whose original family name was probably *Pulcinella,*) first came into existence at Acerra, an ancient city at a short distance from Naples. The date of this event is differently stated by authors who have incidentally mentioned him ; Riccoboni* fixing it before the year 1600, and Gimma† and Signorelli‡ after the commencement of the seventeenth century. The words of Gimma are very precise, and as he enters into particulars, it seems safe to rely upon his authority for this important fact : he says, " Silvio Fiorillo, comedian, who procured himself to be called the Captain Matamoros, invented the Neapolitan Pulcinella; to which Andrea Calcese, who had the sur-name of Ciuccio, by study and natural grace added much. Calcese was a tailor, and died in the plague of the year 1656 : he imitated the peasants of Acerra, a very ancient city of Terra di Lavoro, not far from Naples." Signorelli expressly calls Punch, *un buffone*§ *dell' Acerra ;* and of the

---

* He uses general terms, and his authority is not much to be relied on : " Histoire du Théatre Italien depuis la Decadence de la Comedie Latine, &c."

† " Italia Letterata," vol. 1. p. 196.

‡ "Storia Critica de'Teatri antiche e moderne."—Napoli 1777. It is to be observed, however, that the Dottore Pietro Napoli Signorelli relies for his assertion on the statement of Gimma in his " Italia Letterata." As one proof that Pulcinella was not known before the year 1600, it may be noticed that he is not mentioned by one of the burlesque poets of Italy, who flou-rished anterior to that date, Berni, Molza, Casa, Lasca, &c.

§ Voltaire, in his " Questions sur L'Encyclopedie," thus speaks of the etymology of the Italian word *buffone,* after ridiculing the classical derivation pedantically assigned to it— " Ce mot de *bufon* est reçu depuis longtems chez les Italiens et

Neapolitans in general, he remarks (p. 231), that, " from a certain national vivacity and disposition, they have been at all times distinguished for their talent in imitating the ridiculous on their stages."* Hence more than one of the amusing personages in their impromptu comedies, or *commedie à soggetto*, inserted by Riccoboni among the plates attached to his work, have had their origin in that lively and luxurious capital.†

In order to give a notion of the species of dramatic entertainment in which these various characters, and among them Pulcinella, were engaged, a further short quotation from Signorelli's work will be useful : he is referring to the state of the Italian comedy in the beginning of the seventeenth century. " In general (he says) the public comedians travelled over Italy, representing certain theatrical performances, called comedies of *art*, in contradistinction to comedies of *learning*, recited in the academies and in private dwellings by well-bred actors for their pleasure and exercise. The plan or plot of the fables, they call it, *à soggetto*, was noted down, as well as

---

chez les Espagnols : il signifiait *mimus, scurra, joculator*, mime, farceur, jongleur. Ménage après Saumaise, le dérive de *bocca infiata*, boursouflé ; et en effet on veut dans un boufon un visage rond et la joue rebondie. Les Italiens disent *bufo magro*, maigre boufon, pour exprimer un mauvois plaisant que ne vous fait pas rire."

* Rapin, in his " Reflexions on Modern Poetry," says of the Italians generally, that they are " naturellement comediens," and that they " expriment mieux le ridicule des choses," adding that their language was well adapted to the purpose.

† They are the ancient and modern Harlequin—the ancient and modern Pantaloon—the ancient and modern Doctor— Beltrame di Milano—Scapin—the Italian Capitan—the Spanish Captain—the Neapolitan Scaramouche—Calabrian Giangurgolo —Mezzettin—Tartaglia—the Neapolitan Pulcinella, and Narcisin of Malabergo. In another of his productions, Riccoboni speaks very contemptuously of the " impromptu" comedy, observing that it " ne merite pas un si beau nom, et que l'on devroit plûtót appeller Farce." He afterwards calls it " ancienne et mercenaire," and tells us that it succeeded " la comedic Latine ; foible et immodeste dans son origine, mais plus chaste et plus ingenieuse dans la suite.—" *Reflexions Historiques et Critiques*," &c., 8vo. Paris, 1738.

the substance and distribution of each scene, while the dialogue was left to the will of the representers. Such histrionic farces contained various trivial buffooneries, and different masks were employed in them.

These performances, in which the actor was left to his own talents and discretion in furnishing the dialogue, were once extremely popular throughout Italy; but from the very nature of the representation, it unluckily happens that not a single specimen has been handed down to our time. The few sentences extracted above, we think, will serve to explain a good deal of the supposed mystery of those ancient English "plots," or "platforms" of theatrical representations discovered in Dulwich College; in which the celebrated Tarlton and others were concerned, and which so long puzzled Malone, Steevens, and some of the other commentators on Shakespeare.* Several of the most distinguished actors of that day had travelled in Italy, and were remarkable for their *impromptu;* and Nash, who had been there, in one of his tracts especially terms the famous clown, Kempe, a "harlequin," (a character constantly engaged in such representations) and adds that his fame had extended south of the Alps.†

However, to pursue this topic would lead us away from the object of our present inquiry. We take it for granted, that Silvio Fiorillo invented Pulcinella, and first introduced him as a variety in the list of buffoons required to represent the impromptu comedies of Naples: but, although he may date his separate existence from about the year 1600, it is a matter of much doubt, whether he was not, in fact, only a branch of a family of far greater antiquity. The discovery, in the year 1727, of a bronze statue of a mime, called by the Romans *Maccus,* has indeed led some antiquaries to the conclusion, that he was, in fact, Pulcinella under a different name, but with the same attributes, and among them a hump-back and a large nose.‡ But that the figure was meant for *Maccus* at all seems mere

* See "Malone's Shakespeare," by Boswell, vol. 3, p. 256, &c.
† See the Dedication of his "Almond for a Parrot," printed about the year 1598.
‡ See D'Israeli's "Curiosities of Literature," vol. 3, p. 9.

speculation, and that Pulcinella and *Maccus* had anything
in common, but hump and nose, is at least as questionable.
The Vice, as he was called, of the ancient Moralities was
common, we apprehend, to the early theatrical representations of most countries : his business was to relieve the
weightier part of the performance by his ridiculous actions,
jests, and buffooneries. He was unquestionably the original
of the Clown, or Fool, of the old English Drama ; and we
think the conjecture is at least plausible, that he was the
original also of Harlequin,* and his near relative Pulcinella. The chief appendage of the Vice was a gilt
wooden sword, and this also belonged to the old Clown,
or Fool, not only in England, but abroad. Rabelais,
speaking of certain presents made by Panurge to the fool
Triboullet, says; "Panurge à sa venue luy donna une vessie
de porc, bien enflée et resonnante, à cause des poys qui de-
dans estoient : plus une espée de boys bien dorée; plus, une
petite gibessiere faiete d'une cogue de tortu :"† which we
thus translate for the benefit of such as may not understand
the antiquated French, " Panurge, on his arrival, gave
him a pig's bladder well inflated, and resounding by
reason of the peas that were within it : moreover, a wooden
sword well gilt : moreover, a small pouch, made of a shell
of a tortoise," Those who consult Mr. Douce's " Illustrations," and particularly his essay on the " Clowns and
Fools of Shakespeare," will find that the bladder at the
end of a stick, the gilt wooden sword,‡ and the pouch or
budget, formed part of the equipments of that personage
in this country. The wooden sword directly connects
Harlequin with the ancient Vice, and more modern Fool,§

---

* Riccoboni, "Histoire du Theatre Italien," quotes several authorities, to shew that a Mime like Harlequin was known to the
ancients : he relies chiefly on an expression of Apuleius, *Mimi
centunculo*, with reference to the patch-work dress.

† Chap. 42, edit. 1553.

‡ If this coincidence had occurred to Mr. D'Israeli, he would
not have said (Curiosites of Literature, vol. 3, p. 10, note) that
" the light lath-sword of Harlequin had hitherto baffled his
most painful researches."

§ In Spain he is called the *Gracioso*, and his dress and equipments are nearly the same as they were in England : the mor-

although we have now enjoined him to silence, and have converted the instrument with which of old he cudgelled the Devil, into a talisman to raise him.

- The dress, too, of Harlequin corresponds very much with the *motley* or parti-coloured habit of the clowns of our old dramatic poets. It is true, that the different hues have been arranged with greater regularity, and the patches are of smaller size. The ordinary habiliments of Punch at the present day, preserved by ancient usage, with his pointed fool's-cap, bear a much nearer re-semblance; and this is one circumstance that evidences the strong family-resemblance between the Vice, Harlequin, and Puncinella.* Riccoboni represents the *ancient* Harlequin in a dress composed of patches, as if his ragged clothes had been often mended, and Goldoni speaks of him as originally a poor foolish dolt. There can be little doubt that this was the real origin of the *motley* of the dramatic and domestic fools in former times. They were retained, or were supposed to be retained, by the nobility, commonly out of charity, and one of their ordinary appellations was *Patch*. Cardinal Wolsey had a fool whose parental name has been lost, and he is now only known by the nick-name belonging to his profession.

Upon the continent, to this day, Harlequin is as talkative as ever, even if his jokes are a little less coarse, and his satire kept within narrower bounds. Voltaire, in his *Encyclopedie*† and elsewhere, quotes several capital sayings and aphorisms by Harlequin; but the account that Addison gives of him would hardly lead us to suppose that in his time he possessed so much wit and acuteness.

---

ris-bells and the bladders are particularly mentioned by Cervantes, in his description of the Parliament of Death: "whilst they were thus discoursing, it fell out, that one of the company came toward them, clad for *the Fool* in the play, with morris-bells, and at the end of a stick he had three cows' bladders full blown," &c. Shelton's "Don Quixote," part 2, chap. 11.

* Dr. Johnson, in a note on "Hamlet," (Act 3, Scene 4,) asserts positively, that "the modern Punch is descended from the ancient Vice;" but this opinion is disputed by Mr. Douce, "Illustrations of Shakspeare," vol. 2, p. 251.

† Vol. 4, p. 427, edition 1775.

He tells us that, in Italy, "Harlequin's part is made up
of blunders and absurdities : he is to mistake one name
for another, to forget his errands, to stumble over queens,
and to run his head against every post that comes in his
way. This is all attended with something so comical in
the voice and gestures, that a man who is sensible of the
folly of the part can hardly forbear to be pleased with
it."* Much of this character has been transferred to the
clowns of our pantomimes, since Harlequin was elevated
in station and degraded in understanding.†

Concluding, then, that Punch is one of the *familia
Harlequini*, and that their common parent was the Vice of
the old Moralities, the question arises, to what circumstance he owes the deformity of his figure, and why his
nose, by its length, is rendered so obtrusive a feature ?
We can only answer, that it pleased his inventor, Silvio
Fiorillo, to make him so ; and, perhaps, he did it in some
degree with a view of rendering him more ridiculous, and
to distinguish him more effectually from other characters
of not dissimilar habits and propensities in the *impromptu*
comedies : hence too, probably, the peculiar quality of his
voice, to which Addison alludes. One striking characteristic of Punch is his amorous inclination ; and it is
generally supposed that individuals with the personal
defect for which he is remarkable, are peculiarly " given
to the feminines ;" and the Italian proverb relating to the
length of nose, needs not, if it could, be repeated. Among

---

* Travels, p. 77, edition 1718.

† A good deal has been written on the etymology of the
word Harlequin : it is very clear that the fanciful derivations
from Francis the First's ridicule of *Charles Quint*, and from
M. de *Harlay-quint*, in the reign of Henry III. of France, are
unfounded. The Rev. Mr. Todd quotes a letter of M. Ranlin,
dated 1521, which affords clear evidence that the "*familiam
Harlequini*" was even then " *antiquam ;*" and as early as the
time of Odericus Vitalis, A.D. 1143, the same family is
mentioned as the *familia Herlechini*. This decisive authority,
from its high antiquity, was not known to Mr. Todd. Whether
Harlequinus, or *Herlechinus*, were really the name of any family,
or whether it was a corruption of the old French *arlot*, a cheat,
must still, and perhaps will ever, remain a matter of dispute
among the learned.

Riccobini's plates is one of Giangurgolo of Calabria, and he is represented with a much larger nose than that of Pulcinella.* In the time of Shakespeare, it seems to have been the custom for usurers on the stage to wear large false noses; but, perhaps, it was intended thus to indicate that they were generally of the Jewish persuasion.†

According to Quadrio, in his " Storia d'ogui Poesia" the name of our hero has relation to the length of his nose : he would spell it Pullicinello from *Pulliceno*, which Mr. D'Israeli translates " turkey-cock," an allusion to the beak of that bird. Baretti has it Pulcinella, because that word in Italian means a hen-chicken, whose cry the voice of Punch is said to resemble.—Pollicenello, as it has also been written, in its etymology from *pollice*, " the thumb," goes upon the mistaken presumption that his size was always diminutive, like that of our English worthy, of cow-swallowing memory. The French *Ponche* has been fancifully derived from no less a personage than Pontius Pilate of the old Mysteries, whom, in barbarous times, the Christians wished to abuse and ridicule.‡ If we cannot settle the disputed point, it is very evident, that in future ingenuity and learning will be thrown away in attempting further elucidation.

At what time and in what country **Punch** became a mere puppet as well as a living performer, we have no distinct information; but it is to be inferred, perhaps, that the transmigration first took place in the land of his birth, and after his popularity had been fully established.§ The

---

* And with some reason, if we confide in the statement of Voltaire in his " Encylopedie Art. Bouc."

† See note 21 to the " Jew of Malta," in *Dodsley's Old Plays*, new edition, vol. 8, p. 279. Also vol. 12, p. 396.

‡ Some have supposed that the English name of Punch was a corruption of *paunch*, from the large protuberance in front with which this personage is provided. This is alluded to by Tom Brown, in his " Common Place Book," where he is adverting to Dunton's " Athenians." " As for their skill in etymology, (he says—vol. 3, p. 283, edit. 1744,) I shall instance in two, *viz. surplice*, from *super* and *pelico;* and *Punch*, quasi *paunch*," &c.

§ He was a puppet in France at an early date; and, in 1721,

B

pleasure derived by the lower orders from his performances might lead to the imitation of his manners and actions in little : in the same way, as will be hereafter seen, that the most applauded representations of our own stage, in the reigns of Elizabeth and James, were very soon made the subjects of "motions" or puppet-plays. One man could thus by a little ingenuity, and at a very cheap rate, represent half a dozen or more characters, and the delusion was aided by the peculiar voice given to Punch by artificial means. Ere long he became· the hero of the exhibition ; and other characters, such as Harlequin and Scaramouch, by degrees sunk into insignificance. The last, as well as the Doctor, is still preserved in some of the performances in this country, and we are assured by those who have recently travelled, that the Spanish Captain, the Calabrian with a huge nose, and some others of the personages enumerated by Riccoboni, yet figure in the Italian puppet-shows. In Holland, about ten years ago, we were present at one of the performances of Punch, (there usually called "Tooueelgek," "stage-fool" or "buffoon") in which a number of other characters peculiar to the country, and among them a burgomaster and a Friesland peasant, were introduced.*

Le Sage wrote pieces to be represented by Pulcinella and his wooden coadjutors. Le Sage had previously produced dramas for the Theatre de la Foire, which being silenced in 1721, he and Francisque, his *co-laborateur*, procured puppets instead of living actors. Piron ridiculed their dullness, and, in a piece called " Arlequin Deucalion," introduced Punch laughing, and apparently with some justice, at the want of wit in Le Sage's representations.

* In Germany he is commonly known by the name of *Hanns Wurst* among the lower orders; the literal translation of which is our Jack Pudding, *Hanns* being John or Jack, and *Wurst* a pudding or sausage. He is also called *Polischinel*, and *Hanns Wurst*, used as a generic term for any kind of buffoon.

CHAPTER II.

ORIGIN AND PROGRESS OF PUPPET-PLAYS IN ENGLAND.

BEFORE we proceed farther, it will be necessary to consider, briefly, the antiquity and nature of puppet-plays in this country. It is the more proper to do so, because they form a branch of our drama which has never been examined by the historians of our stage with as much interest and industry as the subject deserves. When we mention that no less a man than Dr. Johnson was of opinion, that puppets were so capable of representing even the plays of Shakspeare, that Macbeth might be performed by them as well as by living actors;[*] it will be evident from such a fact only, that the inquiry is far from unimportant. In connection with this opinion, and confirmatory of it, we may add, that a person of the name of Henry Rowe, shortly before the year 1797, did actually by wooden figures, for a series of years, go through the action of the whole of that tragedy, while he himself repeated the dialogue which belongs to each of the characters.[†]

Puppet-plays are of very ancient date in England ; and, if they were not contemporary with our Mysteries, they probably immediately succeeded them. There is reason to think that they were coeval, at least, with our Moralities; and, in Catholic times, it is not a very violent supposition

---

[*] See Malone's " Shakspeare," by Boswell, vol. 11, p. 301.

[†] He was also called the York Trumpeter, having been born in that city, and having " blown a battle blast" at Culloden. He was born in 1726, and after the Rebellion he retired to his native place ; where, for about fifty years, he graced with his instrument the entrance of the Judges twice a year into York. He was a very well known character, and for a long time before his death in 1800, was master of a puppet-show. In 1797, he

to conclude that the Priests themselves made use even of the images of the Saints and Martyrs, perhaps for this very purpose : it is well ascertained, not only that they did not scruple to employ the churches, but that those sacred edifices were considered the fittest places for our earliest dramatic representations.*

" Motion" is the most general term by which they are mentioned by our ancient authors, and especially by our dramatists : thus Shakspeare, in the " Winter's Tale" (Act 4, Scene 2) makes Autolycus say : " Then he compassed a *motion* of the Prodigal Son, and married a tinker's wife within a mile of where my land and living lies." It would be easy to multiply quotations to the same point from nearly all his contemporaries, but one is as good as a thousand. The nature and one method of their representation at that period, and doubtless long before, may be seen at the close of Ben Jonson's " Bartholomew Fair." He there makes Lanthern Leatherhead convert the story of Hero and Leander (then very popular from Marlow's and Chapman's translation, or rather paraphrase of it), into a " motion" or puppet-play ; and he combines with it the well-known friendship of Damon and Pythias, a story long before dramatised. The exhibitor, standing above and working the figures, " interprets" for them, and delivers the burlesque dialogue he supposes to pass between the characters. In the same Poet's " Tale of a Tub," (Act. 5) In-and-in Medley presents a " motion" for the amusement of the company, connecting it with the plot of the comedy itself. Here he explains the scenes as he proceeds, something in the manner of the ancient Dumb-shows before the

---

published his edition of " Macbeth," with new notes and various emendations. At his decease, the following lines, never yet printed, were written upon him :

" When the great Angel blows the judgment trump,
    He also must give Harry Rowe a thump :
    If not, poor Harry never will awake,
    But think it is his own trumpet, by mistake.
    He blew it all his life, with greatest skill,
    And but for want of breath had blown it still."

* See the new edition of " Dodsley's Old Plays," vol. 1, p. 43, *et seq.*

different acts of " Ferrex and Porrex," the " Misfortunes of
Arthur," and other old tragedies,* but the puppets are not
represented as speaking among themselves. Ben Jonson
may always be relied on in matters relating to the customs
and amusements of our ancestors, as he was a very
minute observer of them ; and from his evidence, we may
infer, that there were, at least, two varieties in the puppet-
plays of his time, one with the dialogue, as in " Bartholomew
Fair ;" and the other without it, but with a descriptive
accompaniment, as in the " Tale of a Tub."†

It is evident, from many passages in our old writers
that might be adduced if necessary, that " motions" were
very popular with the lower orders ; they frequently
rivalled and imitated the performers on the regular stages.
Hence, perhaps, a portion of the abuse with which they
were commonly assailed by some of our dramatic poets,
who were of course anxious to bring them as much as
possible into contempt. It is established, on the authority
of Dekker, and other pamphleteers and play-writers of
about the same period, that the subjects of the " villanous
motions" were often borrowed from the most successful
dramatic entertainments. Shakspeare's "Julius Cæsar," was
performed by *mammets*, (another term in use for the wooden
representatives of heroes,) as well as the " Duke of Guise,"
a name that was perhaps given to Marlow's " Massacre of
Paris,‡" or it may refer to a tragedy by Webster under

---

* These dumb-shows have been thought peculiar to our
elder stage, on the first rise of tragedy ; but R. Brome employs
the same expedient of conveying information on the progress
of the story in his " Queen and Concubine," which was printed in
1659.   During the progress of it, a supernatural character,
called " a genius," explains what is passing, much in the same
way as the owner of " a motion" interpreted for his figures.

† The manner in which puppet-shows were represented in
Spain, is very clearly described in chap. 26 of the second
part of " Don Quixote." Peter there worked the figures, and
his boy interpreted, though not to the knight's satisfaction.
The fable in that instance was purely romantic, but sacred
subjects were at least as common.

‡ Henslowe probably refers to this play, as " the tragedy of
the Guyes," in his papers. See " Malone's Shakespeare,"
by Boswell, vol. 3, p. 299.

that title.* If inference were not sufficient, testimony
might be adduced to shew that the puppets were clothed
as nearly as possible like the actors at the regular theatres
in those plays which were thought fit subjects for the
" motions." The minute fidelity of Ben Jonson to the
manners of his day, in depicting the " humours" of his
characters, has led him in several places to introduce the
name of a principal proprietor of puppet-shows, who was
known by the title of Captain Pod. He mentions him in
his " Every Man out of his Humour,"† as well as in his
" Epigrams,"‡ from which last it also appears that the word
" motion," which properly means the representation by
puppets, was sometimes applied to the figures employed
in the performance.§

The formidable rivalship of puppet-plays to the regular
drama at a later date is established by the fact, that the
proprietors of the theatres in Drury Lane, and near Lincoln's
Inn Fields, formerly petitioned Charles II. that a puppet-
show stationed on the present site of Cecil Street in the
Strand, might not be allowed to exhibit, or might be
removed to a greater distance, as its attractiveness
materially interfered with the prosperity of their concerns.
It is not unlikely that burlesque and ridicule were some‧
times aimed at the productions of the regular stage by the
exhibitors of "motions."

There is little doubt that the most ancient puppet-shows,
like the Mysteries, dealt in stories taken from the Old and
New Testament, or from the lives and legends of Saints.
Towards the end of the reign of Elizabeth, as we have seen,
historical and other fables began to be treated by them;
but still scriptural subjects were commonly exhibited, and

---

* See the Dedication to Webster's " White Devil," as quoted
in note,‡ in the new edition of "Dodsley's Old Plays,"vol. 6, 207.

† " Nay rather let him be Captain Pod, and this his motion,
for he does nothing but shew him." (Act 4, scene 4.)

‡ The title of the Epigram is " On the new motion"—
    "See you yond' motion? not the old fa-ding,
        Nor Captain Pod, nor yet the Eltham thing," &c.

§ Thus also *Speed*, in the " Two Gentlemen of Verona," ex‑
claims, " O excellent *motion!* O exceeding *puppet!* now will
he *interpret* to her." (Act 2, scene 1.)

Shakespeare, in the quotation we have made from his "Winter's Tale," mentions that of the "Prodigal Son." Perhaps, none was more popular than "Nineveh, with Jonas and the Whale :" it is noticed by Ben Jonson twice in the same play, ("Every Man out of his Humour,") and not less than twenty other authors speak of it. From a passage in Cowley's "Cutter of Coleman Street," (Act 5, sc. 2,) we collect that even the Puritans, with all their zealous hatred of the "profane stages," did not object to be present at its "holy performance." The motion of "Babylon" is also frequently noticed ; but "London" and "Rome" likewise figured in the metropolis at the same time, Fleet street and Holborn Bridge, both great thoroughfares, were the usual places where puppet-plays were exhibited in the reign of Elizabeth ;* and the authority of Butler has been quoted by Mr. Gifford (Ben Jonson, v. 2, 46, note) to show that Fleet Street continued to be infested by "motions" and "monsters" at least down to the Restoration. Scriptural motions were not wholly laid aside within the last fifty or sixty years; and Goldsmith, in his comedy, "She Stoops to Conquer," refers to the display of Solomon's Temple in a puppet-show. The current joke (at what date it originated seems uncertain) of Punch popping his head from behind the side curtain, and addressing the Patriarch in his ark, while the floods were pouring down, with "hazy weather, master Noah,"† proves that, at one period, the adventures of the hero of comparatively modern exhibitions of the kind were combined with stories selected from the Bible.

The late Mr. Joseph Strutt, in his "Sports and Pastimes of the People of England," thus speaks of the puppet-shows in his time. "In my memory these shows consisted of a wretched display of wooden figures, barbarously formed and decorated, without the least degree of

---

* *Motions* were also frequently exhibited at Brentford. Mayne, and other old dramatists, speak of city wives going thither to see them.

† This might very well belong to Piron's "Arlequin Deucalion," mentioned in a note in the preceding chapter. Perhaps the joke was derived from thence.

taste or propriety : the wires that communicated the motion to them appeared at the top of their heads, and the manner in which they were made to move evinced the ignorance and inattention of the managers. The dialogues were mere jumbles of absurdities and nonsense, intermixed with low immoral discourses, passing between Punch and the fiddler, for the orchestra rarely admitted of more than one minstrel ; and these flashes of merriment were made offensive to decency by the actions of the puppet."*

From whatever cause the change may have arisen, certain it is, that, at present, in the ordinary exhibitions of " Punch and Judy," the breaches of decorum complained of by Mr. Strutt are rare and slight. He afterwards proceeds as follows : " In the present day, the puppet-show-man travels about the streets, when the weather will permit, and carries the motions, with the theatre itself, upon his back. The exhibition takes place in the open air, and the precarious income of the miserable itinerant depends entirely on the voluntary contribution of the spectators, which, as far as one may judge from the squalid appearance he usually makes, is very trifling."

We have never seen less than two men concerned in these ambulatory exhibitions : one to carry the theatre and use Punch's tin whistle, and the other to bear the box of puppets and blow the trumpet. During the performance the money is collected from the bystanders : the " squalid appearance" of the proprietors is part of their business, and, far from agreeing with Mr. Strutt that the contributions are " very trifling," we have seen, for we have taken the pains to ascertain it, two or three and four shillings obtained at each repetition ; so that supposing only ten performances take place in a summer's day, the reward to the two men on an average might be about fifteen shillings each. On one occasion, we remember to have seen three different spectators give sixpence, besides the halfpence elsewhere contributed : on which the collector went back to the theatre and whispered the exhibitor,

---

* Page 152, edit. 1810. We are glad to see that a new edition of this learned and entertaining work is about to be printed in a convenient 8vo. form, under the care of Mr. Hone.

who immediately made Punch thus address the crowd :
" Ladies and Gentlemen, I never yet played for sevenpence
halfpenny, and I never will ; so good morning."   He then
" struck his tent" and departed ; pocketing nearly two
shillings, and excusing himself from going through the
performance, under pretence that all the contributions he
had received only amounted to sevenpence halfpenny.

CHAPTER III.

ARRIVAL OF PUNCH IN ENGLAND.

WE now come to a point of great national importance—when Punch made his *début*, or first appearance, in England. Great events are usually recorded on the page of history, but this is one, that, by some strange fatality, has escaped all notice ; and, after the lapse of more than a century, we have been called upon to examine forgotten records, and to furnish detailed information. The documents in the State Paper Office, the Records in the Tower, the Rolls of Parliament, and the MSS. in the British Museum, and in the Libraries of the Universities, we are sorry to observe, have supplied us with no intelligence regarding Mr. Punch, Mrs. Judy, or any other member of his family. We have also patiently gone through Evelyn's and Pepys's Diaries, with many other works of the same kind, in print and out of print ; but though they dwell on the Fire of London, the Plague, declarations of war, treaties of peace, the reception of ambassadors, and other historical trifles of that sort, they are silent regarding the arrival of this illustrious foreigner.

Dr. Drake, (and a great many writers before him, for he seldom runs the risk of advancing a novelty,) has called the reign of Queen Anne "the Augustan Age of Literature" in England.* Its claim to this proud distinction has been disputed, and certain admirers of old prose and poetry have set up the reign of Elizabeth in opposition to it. Now, although *non nostrum tantas componere lites*, if we can clearly establish, that the puppet-

---

* See his Essays illustrative of the "Tatler," "Spectator," and "Guardian," vol. 1, p. 32.

show of " Punch and Judy" was well known and much admired, while

"Our gracious Anne was Queen of Britain's Isle ·"

if he reached this country a little before that period, and if the refined theatrical entertainment he offered, so well suited to a highly polished and enlightened nation, were then popular, it will, we think, turn the scale at once, and settle the question for ever.*

We find frequent mention of him in the "Tatler," and even the "classical Addison" does not scruple, in the "Spectator," to introduce a regular criticism upon one of the performances of Punch. As the "Tatler," was published earlier in point of date,† we will begin by referring to

---

* We have already seen that Nash mentions Harlequin before the year 1600 ; but we afterwards lose sight of him, by that name, for three quarters of a century. Dryden notices him ; and Ravenscroft, in 1677, reproduced him upon the stage, in a piece called "Scaramouch a Philosopher, Harlequin a School-boy, Bravo, Merchant and Magician." He calls it "a comedy after the Italian manner ;" and in the prologue he professes to have used Moliere's "Fourberies de Scapin,"which he might not have acknowledged, had not Otway been just before-hand with him. However, Ravenscroft had the good sense to adopt the two best scenes of the French play, which Otway omitted, and which Moliere himself borrowed from "de Bergerac." Ravenscroft's play includes not only the Harlequin, but the Doctor, the Scaramouch, and the Captain of the Italian *impromptu* comedy. The latter is called "Spitzaferro," and is described as "a coward, ignorant and bold," of the same species as the Captain Matamoros, (or *Moor-k.ller,*) in which Silvio Fiorillo, the inventor of Pulcinella, was so famous as always to pass by that title. The Spanish Captain was brought upon the stage while the Spaniards had possession of Naples in the end of the 15th and beginning of the 16th centuries ; but, as he was intended to ridicule that nation, of course he originated in some other part of Italy. After 1677, we have no distinct notice of Harlequin in England, until 1719, when a mock-opera called "Harlequin Hydaspes," was acted at Lincoln's Inn Fields Theatre. Cibber, in his "Apology," gives a full account of the use Rich subsequently made of him, in opposition to the regular drama.

† The first number is dated April 12, 1709 : the firs number of the "Spectator" is dated March 1, 1710-11.

the notices of the same notorious and amusing actor by
Sir Richard Steele. Dr. Johnson was one of the first,
if not the very first, to broach the notion that his age had
become to⌐ wise for the periodicals of Queen Anne's
time ;* as if supposing the fact to be so, there was nothing
else to be gained from the lucubrations of the wittiest and
ablest men of that day, but their out-of-date learning.
The effect has been, with the co-operation of no small
share of self-conceit in the present generation, to throw
the best of our essayists far into the shade; and the
"Tatler," "Guardian," and "Spectator," are now considered
works very well for the period at which they were written,
but far behind the rapid " march of intellect" during the
last forty or fifty years. On this account we shall not
content ourselves with bare references, because we are
aware, that many of those who read our pages will not
have the contemned productions we have named within
their reach.

The great exhibitor of Punch immortalized, we will
say, by Steele, notwithstanding the disesteem into which
that delightful writer has fallen, is Mr. Powell; and in
No. 44 of the " Tatler," Isaac Bickerstaff, Esq., complains
that he had been abused by Punch in a Prologue, supposed
to be spoken by him, but really delivered by his master,
who stood behind, " worked the wires," and, by " a thread
in one of Punch's chops," gave to him the appearance of
enunciation. These expressions are important, inasmuch
as they shew a method of performance and a degree of
intricacy in the machinery not now known. At present
the puppets are played only by putting the hand under the
dress, and making the middle finger and thumb serve for
the arms, while the fore-finger works the head. The
opening and shutting of the mouth is a refinement which
does not seem to be practised in Italy; and it will be
seen by a quotation we shall make presently from another
contemporary work, that Powell's puppets were "jointed."
No. 50 of the " Tatler," contains a real or supposed letter
from the showman himself at Bath, insisting upon his right
of control over his own puppets, and denying all know-

---

* See Dr. Johnson's Life of Addison.

ledge of "the original of puppet-shows; and the several changes and revolutions that have happened in them since Thespis." A subsequent number (115) is curious, as it shews that such was the rivalship of Punch in point of attractiveness, particularly with the ladies, that the Opera and the celebrated singer Nicolini were almost deserted in his favour. Nicolini and the Opera were ridiculed, as we find from other sources, by the squeakings of a pig, well instructed for the purpose, and who had been also taught to dance. From the "Tatler" we learn, that then, as now, Punchinello (for he is so designated and dignified) had a " scolding wife," and that he was attended, besides, by a number of courtiers and nobles.

Powell's show was set up in Covent Garden, opposite to St. Paul's Church; and the "Spectator" (No. 14*) contains the letter of the sexton, who complained that the performances of Punch thinned the congregation in the church, and that, as Powell exhibited during the time of prayers, the tolling of the bell was taken, by all who heard it, for notice of the intended commencement of the exhibition. The writer of the paper then proceeds, in another epistle, to establish that the puppet-show was much superior to the opera of " Rinaldo and Armida," represented at the Haymarket, and to observe that "too much encouragement could not be given to Mr. Powell's skill in *motions*." A regular parallel is drawn between the two, which ends most decidedly in favour of Powell in every respect but the inferior point of the moral.†

But the most curious and particular information regarding Powell and his performance, is contained in a small work published in London in 1715, professing to give an account of his life : it is entitled " A Second Tale of a Tub; or the History of Robert Powell, the Puppet-

---

* Attributed to Steele, who had the good taste· to be delighted with Mr. Punch.

† Penkethman, an actor, and the head of a strolling company, often praised for his low humour, in the reign of Anne, seems also at one time to have been master of a puppet-show of some kind; but as so remarkable a personage as Punch is not mentioned, it is supposed that it was confined to an exhibition of the " heathen gods," as noticed in No. 31 of the *Spectator*.

showman;" but it is, in fact, a political satire on Sir Robert Walpole, to whose life and administration nearly all the adventures are made applicable. It is preceded by a copper-plate, in which that celebrated minister, in a court dress, is represented as the master and interpreter of a puppet-show: he stands below, with a stick to point to the different characters; behind is the stage, lighted with foot-lamps, on which stand a male and female puppet, the male having a very lofty conical cap, a large ruff, and a considerable paunch, (but without the long nose which distinguishes Punch); and the female in a very plain dress with a falling band. The Dedication particularly refers to the extreme popularity of Powell, to his exhibitions at Bath, and in Covent Garden, and then proceeds thus :—

" It would be trifling, after this, to recount to you how Mr. Powell has melted a whole audience into pity and tears, when he has made the poor starved *Children in the Wood* miserably depart in peace, and a Robin bury them. It would be tedious to enumerate how often he has made *Punch* the diversion of all the spectators, by putting into his mouth many bulls and flat contradictions, to the dear joy of all true Teagues. Or to what end should I attempt to describe how heroically he makes *King Bladud* perform the part of a British Prince."

In the body of the work, after going through the supposed adventures of Powell, he reduces him at last to a puppet-showman, and thus continues :—

" Now was he (Powell) resolved to get actors that should move and speak as he pleased. The first he hired was one *Punch*, a comical, staring, gaping, noisy fellow. Punch was soon attended by a whole train of diminutive actors, of both sexes, *viz.*, jointed kings, queens, waiting-maids, virgins, babies, noblemen, baboons, tumblers, aldermen, rope-dancers, geese, country squires, rats, lord mayors, footmen, sows, Indians, cats, conjurors, owls, priests, brazen heads, robin-redbreasts, and elders, all of which were assisted by a wise interpreter; so Mr. Powell had quickly a full stage. In short he was mightily frequented by all sorts of quality, and Punch with his gang soon broke the strollers, and enjoyed the city of Bath by themselves. Money coming in apace, Mr. Powell bought him several new scenes, for the diversion of his audience and the better acting of several incomparable dramas of his own composing, such as ' Whittington and his Cat,' ' The Children in the Wood,' ' Dr. Faustus,' ' Friar Bacon and Friar Bungay,' ' Robin Hood and Little John,' ' Mother Shipton,' ' Mother Goose,' together with the pleasant and comical humours of Valentini, Nicolini, and the tuneful warbling pig, of Italian race."

Nearly all the humour of the application to Sir Robert Walpole, of the " Second Tale of a Tub," is now lost; but the anonymous author seems to have possessed some wit, and was much better acquainted with the ancient as well as modern drama of this country than most of his contemporaries.

From these sources we collect, most distinctly, that the popularity of Punch was completely established, and that he triumphed over all his rivals, materially lessening the receipts at least at the Opera, if not at the regular national theatres; and accomplishing, at that period, by his greater attractiveness, what Dennis, by his " Essay on Operas after the Italian manner," and other *critiques de profession* had been unable to effect. He could hardly have taken such firm possession of the public mind if he had only recently emigrated from his native country; and no writer of the reign of Queen Anne, who notices him at all, speaks of him as a novelty. This may be established from poetry as well as prose. Gay, in his " Shepherd's Week—Saturday," distinguishes between the tricks of " Jack Pudding in his parti-coloured jacket," and " Punch's feats," and tells us that they were both well known at rustic wakes and fairs: but perhaps the most remarkable account of our hero is to be found among Swift's humorous political pieces, in " A Dialogue between mad Mullinix and Timothy," regarding which personages it is not necessary for us to insert explanations which may easily be found elsewhere. A description of a puppet-show, as it then was exhibited, is introduced by way of illustration; and from our extract (with one omission only, for the sake of decorum), it will be seen that it possessed the recommendation of extraordinary variety.

" Observe, the audience is in pain
While Punch is hid behind the scene,
But when they hear his rusty voice,
With what impatience they rejoice !
And then they value not two straws
How Solomon decides the cause ;
Which the true mother,—which pretender,
Nor listen to the witch of Endor.
Should Faustus, with the Devil behind him,
Enter the stage, they never mind him ;
If Punch, to stir their fancy, shews
In at the door his monstrous nose,
Then sudden draws it back again,
Oh ! what a pleasure mix'd with pain !
You every moment think an age,
Till he appears upon the stage :
And first himself you see him clap
Upon the Queen of Sheba's lap.
The Duke of Lorraine drew his sword :
Punch roaring ran, and running roar'd,
Reviles all people in his jargon,
And sells the King of Spain a bargain :
St. George himself he plays the wag on,
And mounts astride upon the dragon :
He gets a thousand thumps and kicks,
Yet cannot leave his roguish tricks ;
In every action thrusts his nose,—
The reason why no mortal knows.
There's not a puppet made of wood
But what would hang him, if they could ,
While, teazing all, by all he's teaz'd,
How well are the spectators pleas'd;
Who in the *motion* have no share,
But purely come to hear and stare ;
Have no concern for Sabra's sake
Which gets the better, saint or snake,
Provided Punch, for there's the jest,
Be soundly maul'd and plague the rest."*

---

* If the curious reader wishes for it, he will find a history of
this poem in the eighth number of the " Intelligencer."

How Punch, King Solomon, Dr. Faustus,* the Queen of Sheba, the Duke of Lorraine, St. George, and the rest of the characters, were brought together, we have no precise knowledge ; but "time and space" were evidently "annihilated, to make *spectators* happy." No wonder that such exhibitions thinned the theatres, and kept the churches empty.

Although our information may be considered complete, as to the high favor in which Punch was then held by the multitude, we are still, and shall probably remain, without any positive intelligence regarding the exact date when he arrived in England. We think, nevertheless, that we may conclude from all the premises with tolerable safety, that he and King William came in together, and that the Revolution is to be looked upon as the era of the introduction of the illustrious Family of Punch, and of the "glorious House of Orange."† Certain it is that the Dutch were extremely celebrated for their skill in mechanics ; and the author of the "Second Tale of a Tub," 1715, bears witness, in the Dedication, "that the Dutch were the most expert nation in the world for puppet-shows."

That the dress and appearance of Punch, in 1731, were as nearly as possible like what they now are, will be seen by the following popular song, extracted from vol. 6 of

---

* Many authorities might be adduced to shew that Dr. Faustus often formed a member of the puppet company. See Pope's "Dunciad," vol. 3, 1. 307 ; C. Pitt's "Prologue to the Strollers ;" A. Hill's "Answer to an Epistle from Mrs. Robinson," &c. According to the author of the "Second Tale of a Tub," one of Powell's shows was called "Doctor Faustus ;" and Mountford, the actor, produced a farce under the same title in 1697.

† There is, however, a passage in Grainger's Biog. Hist. vol. 4, 350, which, if taken literally, as perhaps it is not meant to be, would shew that Punch was known in England before the abdication of James II. He is speaking of a notorious Merry-Andrew, of the name of Phillips, who, he says, "was some time fiddler to a puppet-show, in which capacity he held many a dialogue with *Punch*, in much the same strain as he did afterwards with the mountebank Doctor, his master, on the stage. This Zany being regularly educated, had confessedly the advantage of his brethren."

C

" The Musical Miscellany," printed in that year.*· In
other respects it is a curious production, and, perhaps, was
sung by Punch himself, in one of his entertainments.   It
is inserted under the title of——

PUNCHINELLO.

Trade's awry, so am I
    As well as some folks that are greater ·
But by the peace we at present enjoy
    We hope to be richer and straighter.
Bribery must be laid aside,
    To somebody's mortification :
He that is guilty, oh, let him be tried,
    And expos'd for a rogue to the nation.
        I'm that little fellow
        Call'd Punchinello,
Much beauty I carry about me ;
    I'm witty and pretty,
    And come to delight ye ;
You cannot be merry without me.
My cap is like a sugar-loaf,
And round my collar I wear a ruff ;
I'd strip and shew you my shape in buff,
        But fear the ladies would flout me.
My rising back and distorted breast,
Whene'er I shew 'em, become a jest ;
And, all in all, I am one of the best,
        So nobody need doubt me.
Æsop was a monstrous slave,
    And waited at Xanthus's table ;
Yet he was always a comical knave,
    And an excellent dab at a fable.

---

* In 1735, was published the third edition of " Harlequin
Horace, or the Art of Modern Poetry," dedicated to the celebrated
John Rich ; one object of which is to shew that Pantomime had
driven poetry from the stage.   A frontispiece represents Harlequin and Punch uniting their efforts to expel Apollo, who,
with his lyre, is making his *exit* from the theatre, Punch giving
the god a parting kick.   The dress of Punch is very nearly the
same as at present, with the exception of the conical hat, which
has a sort of brim to it.

So when I presume to show
  My shape, I am just such another;
By my sweet looks and good humour, I know,
  You must take me for him or his brother.
    The fair and the comely
    May think me but homely,
  Because I am tawney and crooked;
    But he that by nature
    Is taller and straighter,
  May happen to prove a blockhead.

But I, fair ladies, am full as wise,
As he that tickles your ears with lies,
And think he pleases your charming eyes
    With a rat-tail wig and a cockade:
I mean the bully that never fought,
Yet dresses himself in a scarlet coat,
Without a commission—not worth a groat,—
    But struts with an empty pocket.

It deserves remark, that Punch has not always been a
mere puppet in the British empire; for in the "Biographia
Dramatica" there is an entry of a farce called "Punch turned
Schoolmaster," which we have not been able to obtain, and
therefore cannot speak of the nature or conduct of it. The
date of its representation is not ascertained, but a prologue
for it was written by Sheridan, and printed in 1724. The
performances of M. Mazurier in 1825, in the " Shipwreck
of Pulcinella, or the Neapolitan Nuptials," are so well
remembered, that it is needless to do more than allude to
them.

CHAPTER IV.

NATURE OF PUNCH'S PERFORMANCES.

WHAT was the dialogue of any of the pieces in which Pulcinella originally performed, soon after his invention, cannot now be distinctly ascertained. We have already seen that they were called *commedie à soggetto* and *commedie all'improviso*, or *impromptu* and *extempore* comedies, the plot and arrangement of which were first communicated to the actors, who afterwards filled up the dialogue according to their own notions, as their wit or invention might serve them.* The schemes, or, as the Italians call them, *canevas* and *scenarie*, of some pieces of this description were printed early in the 16th century, by Flamineo Scala, and others, appeared in 1661, but not a syllable of what passed between any of the characters is there supplied. Hence almost everything must depend upon conjecture; but the probability certainly is, that actors of this class, accustomed repeatedly to perform together, would, ere long, come to a perfect understanding with each other, and the interlocutions thus acquire a certain degree of permanence, until some change took place in the company.† At different places the same

---

* The Reader who wishes for further knowledge upon this subject, may either consult D'Israeli's Curiosities of Literature, vol. 3, 25, or the authorities from which he derived his statements, Gimma's "Italia Letterata," Signorelli's "Storia Critica de Teatri," &c., and Riccoboni.

† Ruzzante was a very famous comedian in the opening of the 16th century, and printed various comedies and dialogues, which he set down from his own invention and from the mouths of the extempore performers (of whom he was one) as the language became habitual: he is mentioned as the first who put different Italian dialects into the mouths of his performers.

plot would be represented, and, of course, the same dialogue would be sufficient, as far as it would be remembered. No doubt, the dramas consisted of " gross buffooneries," because the actors were *buffone ;* but there was room for the display of ready talent; and if a few of the pieces had been left upon record, we should most likely have found that they had something else to recommend them besides the coarseness of their jokes, delivered in the dialect of Italy peculiar to each of the characters.*

" Il Travaglia," by Andrea Calmo, printed at Venice in 1557, also professes to be *di varie lingue adornata.* Riccoboni informs us that Scaramouche, Harlequin, and other characters, threw off their provincialism on occasion, and *tous declament des vers en bon Romain.*

* The actors, whether representing the Neapolitan " Pulcinella," the Calabrian " Giangurgolo," or the Milanese " Beltrame," preserved the dialect of their respective countries. The Spanish Captain spoke a language compounded of Italian and Spanish. Of the dialect employed by Punch, and by the country people of Acerra, (of whom he was originally supposed to be one,) we have a specimen in a three-act comedy, called " Puncinella finto Dottore," which was acted at Rome during the Carnival of 1728. A very short extract will suffice, as the language is sometimes scarcely intelligible to a native. FLAMINEO, a young lover, is endeavouring to persuade his servant, PULCINELLA, to assume the dress and appearance of DOCTOR FARFALLONE, his rival, in order to impose upon the father of the lady.

FLAM. E possibile, che non ti dia l'animo di dire queste quattro parole?

PUL. Ne diraggio cinquanta, bene mio, mà se tu struppei do discurso.

FLAM. E come dirai?

PUL. Diraggio cà songo venuto dalla Cierra per nzorarme.

FLAM. E ti chiami?

PUL. Purcenella.

FLAM. O stordito! ed ecco atterrata tutta la machina.

PUL. E peche?

FLAM. E perche tu hai du dire che sei il Dottore, venuto da Bologna, e ti chiami Farfallone.

PUL. E ca non buoglio rinega lo pajeso mio, e poi chillo nome de Farfantone non c'aggio genio nente, cà fete no tantillo di galera, &c.

Neither in England have we the means of knowing with precision, the nature of the earlier exhibitions of " Punch and his merry family." How the stories of Mr. Powell were compounded, as far as relates to the dialogue, must remain a mystery, the writers of his day never entering into this interesting point. It appears from the "Spectator" (No. 14), that under the little Piazza, in Covent Garden, Mr. Powell's hero danced a minuet with " a well-disciplined pig; which, according to the " Second Tale of a Tub," had been taught also to ridicule the celebrated Italian singers, Valentini and Nicolini; and in the same show, " King Harry (probably the Eighth) laid his leg upon the Queen's lap in too ludicrous a manner." We likewise learn on this authority, as well as from Swift, that, at that time, Punch possessed the same animating voice which, when heard in our streets, still lights up the eyes of the rising generation.

The Spectator, and the " Second Tale of a Tub," may further be brought forward, to prove that " Whittington and his Cat"* was one of the subjects chosen by Mr. Powell for the display of his talents. We take it for granted, that in all these cases, as at the present moment, the dialogue was extemporaneous, excepting in so far as it became habitual and mechanical by frequent repetition. That singing then formed part of the entertainment, is not mere matter of inference, and we know that it did so in the time of Strutt, who also speaks of a fiddler, now discon-

---

* It has, we believe, been hitherto thought that the story of " Whittington, thrice Lord Mayor of London," was exclusively national; but supposing the notion to be well founded, what we are about to mention affords one more proof to those already furnished of late years, that, in time, tales of the kind become the common property of other countries. It is found among the " Facezie, Motti, Buffonerie, et Burle" of the Piovano Arlotto, which were originally printed very early in the 16th century, and subsequently were re-issued from the celebrated press of the Giunti, at Florence, in 1565. The title it there bears is this : " Il Piovano, à un prete che fece mercantia di palle, dice la novella delle gatte." With a change of persons and places, it is the same story as our own " Whittington and his Cat."

tinned : many living can remember the introduction of
" snatches of old songs," and parodies of popular ballads
by Punch. Steele makes mention of Powell's " books;"
but, in all likelihood, they were not books of his perform-
anecs, which in our day, and for our purpose, would be
great curiosities.

At all events, there is certain ground for concluding
that the adventures of Punch, as represented in this
country, did not by any means always consist of that
series in which they are now usually performed; and
although we are not in a condition to adduce distinct
proof upon the point, we cannot help thinking that the
introduction and popularity of " Don Juan" contributed
mainly to the arrangement of the performance as it is
now daily exhibited.* We have consulted some persons
whose age is sufficiently advanced to enable them to
supply the information, and they agree that about that
period the character of Punch certainly underwent a
material change. Although we are inclined to favour
this hypothesis, we must allow that the story, as displayed on some parts of the continent at the present
moment, bears many features of strong resemblance to
the fable of the piece as shewn in Great Britain.† We
here advert to Punch in the puppet-show, and not on the
stage in Italy.

The original of " Don Juan" is generally allowed to
be Spanish : in that language, it is called *Il Convidado di
Pietra*, and its author was Tirso de Molina. It was played

---

* Hone, in his account of the " Mysteries," &c. draws a
parallel between the two; but, in order to render it more
obvious, he a little perverts the story of Punch, particularly
in the catastrophe.

† It seems hardly likely that this change was earliest effected
in Italy; for when Goldoni brought out his " Don Juan," he for
the first time left out Harlequin, and introduced other comic
characters in his place, as he himself informs us in his Memoirs
(vol. 1, p. 311, edit. Paris, 1787.) In the *Convidado di Pietra*, to
which the Italians had been accustomed, Harlequin on one occasion saves himself by swimming, with the aid of a couple of
bladders. Sacchi was the most famous Harlequin of his day,
and is highly extolled by Goldoni, who wrote several pieces
expressly for him.

in Paris first by the Italian company; and to rival them
an actor of the name of Villiers brought it out in French
verse, at another theatre, while the biographers of
Moliere informs us that he wrote his *Festin de Pierre* in
prose, because he was in such haste to anticipate Villiers.
T. Corneille added rhymes to it on the death of Moliere.
Three years afterwards, *viz.* in 1676, it first appeared on
the English stage, from the pen of Shadwell; but Punch
was, probably, then unknown here, at least by that appel-
lation, and the change in the fable, to which we have
referred, was occasioned, if at all, long afterwards, by the
extreme popularity of the pantomine-ballets at the Royalty, and subsequently at Drury Lane Theatre, about
forty years ago.*

The ensuing ballad was written very nearly about that
date, being extracted from a curious collection of comic
and serious pieces of the kind, in print and manuscript,
with the figures 1791, 1792, and 1793, in various parts
of it, as the times, probably, when the individual who
made it obtained the copies he transcribed, or inserted in
their original shape.   It certainly affords evidence of the
connection between the stories of Punch and Don Juan;
and (like the old ballads of "King Lear and his Three
Daughters," "The Spanish Tragedy, or the lamentable
murder of Horatio and Bellimperia," &c.) was perhaps
founded upon the performance, by one who had witnessed
and was highly gratified by it.   It is called,

PUNCH'S PRANKS.

Oh! hearken now to me awhile,
    A story I will tell you
Of Mr. Punch, who was a vile
    Deceitful murderous fellow :
Who had a wife, a child also,—
    And both of matchless beauty;
The infant's name I do not know,
    Its mother's name was Judy.
            Right tol de rol lol, &c.

---

* "Don Juan" was acted at the Royalty Theatre in 1787,
and at Drury Lane in 1790.   It was played many nights
in succession, and are hardly yet laid aside.

But not so handsome Mr. Punch,
   Who had a monstrous nose, sir;
And on his back there grew a hunch
   That to his head arose, sir:
But then, they say, that he could speak
   As winning as a mermaid;
And by his voice—a treble squeak—
   He Judy won—that fair maid.

But he was cruel as a Turk ·
   Like Turk, was discontented,
To have one wife—'twas poorish work—
   But still the law prevented
Ilis having two, or twenty-two,
   Though he for all was ready ·
So what did he in that case do?
   Oh! sad!—he kept a lady.

Now Mrs. Judy found it out,
   And, being very jealous,
She pull'd her husband by the snout,
   His lady gay as well as.
Then Punch he in a passion flew,
   And took it so in dudgeon,
He fairly split her head in two
   Oh! monster!—with a bludgeon.

And next he took his little heir—
   Oh, most unnatural father!—
And flung it out of a two-pair
   Window; for he'd rather
Possess the lady of his love,
   Than lady of the law, sir;
And cared not for his child above
   A pinch of Maceaban, sir.

His wife's relations came to town
   To ask of him the cause, sir;
He took his stick and knock'd 'em down
   And serv'd 'em the same sauce, sir.

And said the law was not *his* law,
  He car'd not for a letter;
And if on him it laid its claw,
  He'd teach it to know better.

Then took to travel o'er each land,
  So loving and seductive,
Three ladies only could withstand
  His lessons most instructive.
The first, a simple rustic maid;
  The next, a pious abbess;
The third I'd call, but I'm afraid,
  The tabbiest of tabbies.*

In Italy, the dames were worst;
  In France, they were too clamorous;
In England, altho' coy at first,
  Yet after quite as amorous.
In Spain, they all were proud, yet frail;
  In Germany, but coolish;
But further north he did not sail,
  To do so had been foolish.

---

* In this stanza, the writer (we regret that so pleasant an effusion should be anonymous) seems to have had in his mind Spenser's Squire of Dames ("Fairy Queen," Book 3, canto 7), who had been commanded by his mistress to go forth a "colonelling" against the virtue of the female sex. He returned in less than a year, with tokens of three hundred conquests; and she then set him a penance to bring testimonies of as many women who had resisted his arts and entreaties. In three years he had only found three.

  " The first which then refused me," said he,
    " Certes was but a common courtesane,
  Yet, flat refused to have a-do with me,
    Because I could not give her many a Jane."
  (Thereat full heartily laugh'd Satyrane.)
    " The second was an holy nun to chose,
  Which would not let me be her chapelaine.
    Because she knew, she said, I would disclose
    Her counsel, if she should her trust in me repose."

  " The third a damsel was of low degree,
    Whom I in country cottage found by chance, &c."

In all his course he scrupled not
    To make a jest of murder,
So fathers, brothers, went to pot :—
    It really makes one shudder
To think upon the horrid track
    Of blood he shed on system ;
And, though with hump upon his back,
    The dames could not resist him.

'Tis said, that he a compact sign'd
    With one they call " Old Nich'lass ;"
But if I knew them, I've no mind
    To go into partic'lars.
To it, perhaps, he ow'd success
    Wherever he might go, sir ;
But I believe we must confess,
    The ladies were so so, sir.

At last he back to England came,
    A jolly rake and rover,
And pass'd him by another name,
    An *alias*, when at Dover.
But soon the police laid a scheme,
    To clap him into prison :
They took him, when he least could dream
    Of such a fate as his'n.*

And now the day was drawing near,
    The day of retribution ;
The trial o'er, he felt but queer
    At thought of execution.
But when the hangman, all so grim,
    Declar'd that all was ready,
Punch only tipp'd the wink at him,
    And ask'd after his lady.

---

* This sounds like an ignorant vulgarism ; but it is, in fact, only an abbreviation, *per illipsin*, of *his own*. We find it applied to the pronoun *her* in George Chapman's " Humorous Day's Mirth," a comedy printed in 1599, sign.: G.

" What shall I do at sight of her and *her'n* ?"

Pretending he knew not the use
    Of rope he saw from tree, sir,
The hangman's head into the noose
    He got, while he got free, sir.
At last, the Devil came to claim
    His own; but Punch what *he* meant
Demanded, and denied the same ·
    He knew no such agreement!

"You don't! (the Devil cried:) 'tis. well ·
    I'll quickly let you know it:
And so to furious work they fell
    As hard as they could go it.
The Devil with his pitch-fork fought
    While Punch had but a stick, Sir
But kill'd the Devil,* as he ought.
    Huzza! there's no Old Nick, sir.
                Right tol de rol lol, &c.

In a previous part of this chapter, we have established,
that Dr. Faustus was a principal character in puppet-
shows of that date ;† and every body knows from the old
Romance‡ and from Goethe's Drama, if not from Marlow's

---

* To kill the Devil," and "to drive the Devil into his own
dominions," *cacciar il Diavolo nell' inferno*, meant the same
thing in Italian, as is fully explained in Boccacio, as well as
Sacchetti, (Novel 101,) and in Bandello, (Novel 9, vol. 1, edit.
Venice, 1566.) It is only used in English in its literal sense, and
it is, of course, so to be understood in this ballad. In its figu-
rative application, perhaps no hero, not even Don Juan himself,
oftener was the death of his Satanic Majesty than Punch. More
we cannot say.

† Mountford, the stage Adonis of his day, in 1697, wrote
what was at that time called " a Farce," on the Life and Death
of Dr. Faustus, in which Harlequin and Scaramouch both
figured, but nothing is said of Punch in it. Lee and Jevon,
two distinguished comic performers, took the parts of Harlequin and Scaramouch, and it seems to have met with success,
as, after having been acted in Dorset Gardens, it was revived
at the Theatre in Lincoln's Inn Fields.

‡ An elegant reprint of it, under the care of Mr. Thoms, has
recently made a scarce and curious work very accessible. We

tragedy, that that renowned conjuror had entered into a similar bond with the potentate of the infernal regions. There may be, therefore, some link of connection between Powell's performance and that upon which the preceding ballad has been framed, which in the lapse of a century has been lost. In our day, we hear nothing of such a compact; but the Devil is brought in to carry away the hero to the punishment merited by his boasted crimes. In this respect, we should rather have taken Punch for a Frenchman than an Italian, according to the opinion of old Heyliu; who, speaking of our near neighbours, and of that vanity which, when he wrote, made them vaunt of their vices, exclaims, in a sort of uncharitable rapture, "foolish and most perishing wretches, by whom each several wickedness is twice committed: first in the act, and secondly in the boast!"*

---

will take this opportunity of pointing out an error in the Introduction (p. 8) where Marlow's Tragedy is spoken of as if it had first appeared in 1610. Marlow was killed in 1593, (before the date assigned by Mr. Thoms to "the Second Report of Dr. Faustus," and his play was printed in 1604. We know of no edition in 1610.

* "France painted to the Life"—London, 1656, p. 53. with the motto *Quid non Gallia parturit ingens*. Dante was no great admirer of the French, whom he thinks only just better than the people of Sienna:

────── *Hor fugiammai*
Gente si vand coma la Sanese?
Certo non la Francesca si d' assai.
                                   Inferno, chap. 29.

CHAPTER V

POETICAL justice is a matter upon which the most sagacious critics have insisted; and it cannot be denied that, in the ordinary exhibitions, which go by the name of " Punch and Judy," it is decidedly violated. One great object, as they contend, of dramatic poetry, ought to be to enforce a moral; and if we try the species of scenic representation now under our view by that test, we shall find it unquestionably deficient. It is nevertheless a point capable of dispute, whether people were ever made better or worse by theatrical performances; for instance, whether a single apprentice was ever deterred or reclaimed from vice by all the sombre repetitions of " George Barnwell," at Easter and Christmas. The old lawyer who used to send his clerks to witness every execution, with the admonition, "There, you rogues, go to school and improve,"* took a course which, from the reality of the sight, was likely to be beneficial : but everybody is aware that what is shown at the theatres is nothing but an attempt to impose; and the audience rather sets itself against the endeavour, than is impressed and corrected by the moral. What, in the cant of the profession, is called " illusion," we are satisfied never exists; and the actors are no more believed to be the characters they represent, than the painted trees and castles of the scenery are supposed to consist of rustling foliage and substantial stone. Dr. Johnson says somewhere, that the actor who for a moment could believe that he was Macbeth, and really perpetrated the murders, would deserve to be hanged; and, we may add, that the audience would deserve it too, as accessories,

---

* Tom Brown's Works, vol. 4, p. 116.

for not interfering on behalf of poor Duncan, if they were persuaded that his life was in danger. We admire a landscape for its truth, as a copy from nature, not because we ever imagine that it is the actual view itself, compressed into the compass of some three feet of gilded frame: what we see on the stage is but a succession of views with moving figures, and we like them little or much in proportion as we approach our notions of reality; but always keeping the imitation perfectly distinct from the thing imitated, and approving the former only because it is an imitation.

" Live o'er each scene, and be what we behold,"

is a very good line from Pope; but if there be any " Roman virtue" in the British character, it does owe it to " Cato ;" and it is remarkable that it never was less apparent than at the time when that tragedy was oftenest represented : the littleness of party spirit was never more despicable, or more despicably displayed, than when " Cato" was first produced upon the stage.

As to the puppet-show of " Punch and Judy," it never is looked at by the lowest of the populace, but as a mere joke; and a most effective part of that joke is the ultimate triumph of the hero; without it, the representation would be not only " flat and stale," but " unprofitable." We have seen it so; for we remember a showman, on one occasion, not merely receiving little or no money, but getting lamentably pelted with mud, because, from some scruple or other, he refused to allow the victory over the Devil to Punch. Besides, it may surely deserve consideration, whether, wicked as Punch unquestionably is, the Devil is not the worse offender of the two, and, consequently, the more deserving of punishment. If so, poetical justice is satisfied.

We have before lamented that, as the performances of Punch in this country very much resemble the impromptu comedies of the Italians, no record exists of the dialogue, and, in few instances, of the course and series of the scenery; the fact, most likely, being, that both the one and the other were often altered to suit the convenience of the manager, or the temper and wishes of his auditory. We shall speak of some of these variations presently; and in the mean-time, and before we lose sight of the connection between Don Juan and the personage, who may now be justly called Don Juan of the multitude, we wish to add in this place the only printed account we ever saw of the plot of one of Punch's exhibitions, and which differs from the story of any of the numerous shows we have witnessed. It is given as a sort of theatrical criticism in a letter from a watering-place, and was published in the " Morning Chronicle" of 22nd September, 1813. The narrative is as follows :—

" Mr. Punch, a gentleman of great personal attraction, is married to Mrs. Judy, by whom he has a lovely daughter, but to whom no name is given in this piece, the infant being too young to be christened. In a fit of horrid and demoniac jealousy, Mr. Punch like a second Zeluco, strangles his beauteous offspring. Just as he has com-pleted his dreadful purpose, Mrs. Judy enters, witnesses the brutal havoc, and *exit* screaming; she soon returns, however, armed with a bludgeon, and applies it to her husband's head, " which to the wood returns a wooden sound." Exasperated by jealousy and rage, Mr. Punch, at length, seizes another bludgeon, soon vanquishes his already weakened foe, and lays her prostrate at his feet; then, seizing the murdered infant and the expiring mother, he flings them both out of the window into the street. The dead bodies having been found, police officers enter the dwelling of Mr. Punch, who flies for his life, mounts his steed, and the author, neglecting, like other great poets, the confining unities of time and place, conveys his hero into Spain, where, however, he is arrested by an officer of the terrible Inquisition. After enduring the most cruel tortures with incredible fortitude, Mr. Punch, by means of a golden key, (a beautiful and novel allegory), opens his prison door and escapes. The conclusion of the affecting story is satirical, allegorical, and poetical. The hero is first overtaken by weariness and laziness, in the shape of a black dog, whom he fights and conquers; disease, in the disguise of a physician, next arrests him; but Punch " sees through the thin pretence," and dis-misses the doctor with a few derogatory kicks. Death at length visits the fugitive, but Punch lays about his skeleton carcase so lustily, and makes the bones of his antagonist rattle so musically with a *bastinado*, that " Death his death's blow then received." Last of all comes the Devil; first, under the appearance of a lovely female, but afterwards in his own natural shape, to drag the offender to the infernal regions, in purgatory to expiate his dreadful crimes. Even this attempt fails, and Punch is left trium. phant over Doctors, Death, and the Devil. The curtain falls amid the shouts of the Conqueror, who on his vic. torious staff lifts on high his vanquished foe."

We do not see, exactly, how the whole of such a plot could have been made out in a puppet show, and we can. not avoid thinking, that this critic, like many others, has here found out " meanings never meant," and which could never have entered the head of any ordinary exhibitor.* With the exception of the skeleton, all the other characters are familiar; and only supposing that the writer has a little disturbed the ordinary course of the events, for his own purpose of making out " more than meets the ear" in an allegory, the whole is very easily explained and understood.

The disregard of the unities of Time and Place is com. mon to all the exhibitions of Punch we ever saw or have heard of, in this or any other country; and it may be the boast of Italy, that, while her regular drama wore these burdensome and useless fetters, under the patronage of the higher classes and the learned, they were thrown off in her *commedie à soggetto*, under the patronage of the lower classes and the unlearned. It is not to be sup. posed, however, that in Italy the impromptu comedies

---

* Casti, in his tale " La Pace di Pasquale," (Nov. 43, vol. 3, Edition 1804,) mentions a friar who had *per le buffonerie raro talento*, and who was able, especially, *fare a maraviglia il Pul- cinella.* Mr. D'Israeli also speaks of " a philosopher and a man of fortune," of his acquaintance, who delighted in per- forming " Punchinello's little comedy." We know several in- stances of fathers, who, for the amusement of their families, go through the part of the puppet-show man. • These individuals might have sufficient invention for such a fable, but still it would not be easy to represent it intelligibly by puppets.

filled by the various characters of Pulcinella, Harlequin, Scaramouch, the Doctor, and others, were exhibited only before the rabble of the community : the contrary might be satisfactorily established.   The most dignified and the gravest not unfrequently laid aside their dignity and their gravity ; and, like Leo X., rejoiced in the broadest representations of the buffoons.*   Dr. Moore, who wrote his " View of Society in Italy," 8vo., 1781, confesses that he and the Duke of Hamilton, going to the performance with all possible prejudices against it, were delighted : he especially dwells upon a most ludicrous scene, in which Harlequin made a stammerer bring out a word which had been sticking in his throat for a quarter of an hour, by striking him on the back, as nurses strike a choking infant.†   We have since seen a refined French auditory laugh heartily at the very same incident, the only difference being, that Potier was not dressed as Harlequin, nor Brunet as Pulcinella.

At various periods, the adventures of Punch have been differently represented and misrepresented, and innovations have been introduced, to suit the taste and to meet the events of the day.   One attempt of this sort was made in Fielding's time, in consequence of the extreme popularity of "the Provoked Husband."   He complains ("Tom Jones," Book 12, chap. 5,) that a puppet-show, witnessed by his hero, included "the fine and serious part" of the comedy we have named.   He then proceeds, from the mouth of Jones, to shew its inferiority to the old exhibition of Punch and his wife, (whom he miscalls *Joan*, by some strange forgetfulness,

---

* "To such an extreme was this propensity carried, that his courtiers and attendants could not more effectually obtain his favour than by introducing to him such persons as, by their eccentricity, perversity, or imbecility of mind, were likely to excite his mirth." Roscoe's Leo X. 4, 370, Edition 1827. This author is at a difficulty to account for this " propensity," which is easily explained on the principle of contrast. It is fortunate for his gravity that *Punch and Judy* were not invented in the time of Leo, for the Pope would certainly have kept a puppet-show for his own private amusement.

† Vol. I. p. 258.

although her name has been *Judy*, as the lawyers say, "from time whereof the memory of man runneth not to the contrary,") which gives some offence to "the dancer of wires," who fancied, as he might do very reasonably, that "people rose from his little drama as much improved as they could do from the great."

Of later years, we have witnessed several singular interpolations. After the battle of the Nile, Lord Nelson figured on one of the street-stages, and held a dialogue with Punch, in which he endeavoured to persuade him, as a brave fellow, to go on board his ship, and assist in fighting the French: "Come, Punch, my boy, (said the naval hero,) I'll make you a captain or a commodore, if you like it."—"But I don't like it, (replied the puppet-show hero;) I shall be drowned."—"Never fear that, (answered Nelson;) he that is born to be hanged, you know, is sure not to be drowned." During one of the Elections for Westminster, Sir F. Burdett received equal honour, and was represented kissing Judy and the child, and soliciting Mr. Punch for his vote. "How are you, Mr. Punch? (enquired the Baronet,) I hope you will give me your support."—"I don't know, (answered Punch,) ask my wife. I leave all those things to Mrs. P."—"That is very right, (continued Sir Francis,) what do you say, Mrs. Judy? Bless me! what a sweet little child you have got, I wish mine were like it."—"And so they may be, Sir Francis, (observed Judy,) for you are very like my husband; you have got such a beautiful long nose."—"True, Mrs. Judy; but Lady B. is not like you, (added Sir Francis, kissing her.) A sweet little infant, indeed! I hope it has good health. How are its little bowels?"—"Charmingly, thank you," was the answer; and Judy could not refuse the solicitations of so gallant and kind-hearted a candidate.

At a country fair, we once saw a donkey-race represented by puppets with a great deal of spirit, and we need hardly add, that Mr. Punch* (though not always the most expert horseman) rode the winner, but was cheated out of

---

* See Act 2, Scene 2, of the "Tragical Comedy of Punch and Judy," where the hero is thrown by his horse, Hector.

the prize. It was no uncommon thing, among the showmen *in eyre*, to insert a scene of a street-row: for this purpose they introduce a watch-box with a *Charley* in it, fast asleep. Punch enters tipsy, overturns the " guardian of the night," and finally is taken to the watch-house. This incident is of " Tom and Jerry" origin, and was not used until those heroes figured in the pages of "Life in London." At various times, we have observed characters inserted from popular performances at our theatres: some of our readers may recollect a conference between Blue Beard and Punch, on the mutually interesting topic of a plurality of wives; and Morgiana from " The Forty Thieves," and Grimaldi from "Mother Goose," have danced together before us. We have been present at an interview between Punch and a person no less distinguished than Paul Pry, in which the latter received severe chastisement for "intruding," while the former was enjoying the delightful converse of one of his female acquaintances.

CHAPTER VI.

ON THE CHARACTER OF PUNCH.

PROFESSOR Richardson, of Glasgow, as everybody knows, wrote a series of "Essays on Shakespeare's Dramatic Characters," in which he entered at length into the design of the author, and the manner in which he had accomplished it. Other admirers of the works of the same poet have published separate dissertations on particular personages in his plays, such as Falstaff, Hamlet, &c. It seems to us that Punch, although not drawn by the same "master-hand," merits a similar distinction; and we shall accordingly proceed to offer a few remarks upon his character, as it is displayed in the most approved representations of the present day. Professor Richardson declared, even in his "fifth edition," that his work was unworthy of the public notice" (rather a bad compliment to his many readers), while we, on the contrary, in our first impression contend that our remarks well deserve attention; and we shall "be of the same opinion still," even if "convinced, against our will," that our work will never arrive at an equal degree of popularity.

We are more disposed to offer a few observations on the character of Punch, because upon none of the *dramatis personæ* of Shakespeare's plays has Professor Richardson bestowed a larger space, or a greater degree of labour, than on Richard III. and Sir John Falstaff: to both of these is Punch, in disposition and talents, akin; and he, besides, combines in his own person the deformity of the one* and the obesity of the other. He is, as it were, a combination and concentration of two of the most prominent and original delineations on the stage : as if

> " The force of nature could no farther go :
> To make a third, she joined the other two."

The similarity between Richard and Falstaff, though not very obvious, has been fully established ; and it consists in the intellectual superiority they both possess, and with the exercise of which the first gratifies his ambition, and the last his appetites. It is the possession of the same high talents (in the last instance applied very much to the attainment of the same ends,) which constitutes Punch's chief moral resemblance. The high authority to which we have just alluded lays it down, and, we may say, proves that " the pleasure we receive from the character of Richard is produced by those emotions which arise in the mind, on beholding great intellectual ability employed for inhuman and perfidious purposes."† If we try the character of Punch by this test, shall we not arrive at the identical conclusion? Like the " crook-back prodigy," he is not " shaped for sportive tricks," and

> " wants love's majesty,
> To strut before a wanton, ambling nymph :"

but to compensate for these personal defects, Punch, like

---

* As he was to have " a spice or somewhat more" of Don Juan about him, and as we are told

> " A decent leg is what all ladies like,"

it was not thought expedient by the inventor or inventors of Punch, to represent him with Richard's tibial disfigurement. Punch's legs are not " legs for boots," but legs fit " to make legs with," and to make legs by. We never saw him at any exhibition without a pair, models of their kind, and in showing which he evinced no slight degree of vanity. There is not, at present, such a thing as a good male leg on the stage ; so that Punch may be excused if he is a little ostentatious. Lord Byron calls a delicate hand and a good leg the criterion of good blood; Punch's leg is not so remarkable for "a vulgar quantity of calf," as for the fineness of its ankle, and the general symmetry of its proportions.

† Edition 1797, p. 204.

Richard, has " a tongue shall wheedle with the Devil,"
and he does, in fact, " wheedle with the Devil," to some
purpose. His wit, his ingenuity, his rapid invention of
expedients, or, in two words, his " intellectual ability,"
is employed for " inhuman and perfidious purposes," and
hence the delight we experience during the representation
of those scenes in which his genius is displayed.* We
freely admit that, as far as the moral is concerned, Shakespeare has the advantage of the author of " Punch and
Judy," in both instances : Richard is slain, and Falstaff
dismissed with contempt ; but to this point we have
already adverted in the preceding chapter.

" The desire of gratifying the grosser and lower appetites
is the ruling and strongest principle in the mind of Falstaff."† Only substitute the name of Punch for that of the

---

* We have elsewhere alluded to the possible intentions of
Silvio Fiorillo in giving Punch such a stupendous nose; but
we omitted one reason which may here be assigned, and would
have been the more applicable, had our hero in Italy at all times
possessed the same unrivalled talents he invariably displays in
this country. This reason is contained in the productions of
some of the Burlesque Poets of Italy ; who, however, as we
have before remarked, do not, and could not, mention Punch,
as he was not invented when they most flourished. Ludovico
Dolce has a " capitolo in lode del Naso," highly extolling " un
gran pezzo di naso," and declaring " che l'huomo è degno
d'ogni stima" who is so provided : he afterwards proceeds thus
in point, and that point is not lost in our translation.

> If any man has but a gracious nose,
> I mean a nose in longitude not scanty,
> His brain with wit and fancy overflows.
> Do we not know that the immortal Dante
> Had a huge nose ? and that's the real cause
> He wrote so well.—Ovid, in style so janty,
> And yet so natural, obtain'd applause
> By his great nose, which likewise gave him name:
> Horace and Virgil envied him.—His jaws
> Berni had vainly open'd, to his shame,
> And to the loss of our supreme delight,
> But that his nose was like a torch on flame.

Punch has a similar ornament, and the same causes produce
the same effects.

† Richardson's Essays, 1797, p. 249.

fat, witty, and luxurious knight, and every syllable is equally applicable. A great deal has been written *pro* and *con*, on the question of Falstaff's cowardice, and it now seems agreed by the learned, not "the commentators on Shakespeare,"

> " Deep-vers'd in books and shallow in themselves ·
> Crude and intoxicate, collecting toys
> And trifles for choice matters, worth a sponge ·

But, by those who have some knowledge of the human mind and its operations, that Falstaff is no coward : while he avows "discretion to be the better part of valour," he only avoids situations of danger, not from constitutional fear of them, but because his strong sense revolts at incurring peril were it is needless. As one of our old translators of Horace shrewdly says, in reference to that poet's disappearance at the battle of Philippi, " a soldier is no more bound to fight when he is out of his humour, than an orator to speak when he is out of his wits ; nor is it prudent for a man of wit and learning to have his brains beaten out by one that has none."* Such is precisely the " discretion," which Falstaff commends. Punch, however, is less prudent than Falstaff, and, in some instances, may perhaps, be almost charged with being a little fool-hardy. He is more amorous ; and in seeking to gratify this propensity, he must, of course, be sometimes prepared, like Don Juan, (whom in this respect he resembles,) " to run upon the very edge of hazard." If, in the course of his adventures, Punch be now and then guilty of ridiculous extravagancies, apparently inconsistent with part of the character we have drawn of him, let it be remembered in the words of Pascal, " l'extreme esprit est accusée de la folie, comme l'extreme défaut."

We have it upon very high and ancient authority, that "no bad man can be happy,"† and, if this maxim be true, the character of Punch is so far out of nature : he hardly knows a moment's unhappiness, from the beginning to the

---

* Alexander Broome's " Life of Horace," prefixed to " The Poems of Horace," &c. by several hands." London, 1666.

† Nemo malus fœlix, &c. Juvenal Satires, iv.

end of his career, scarcely excepting even the period of his confinement before he is led out to execution. Punch, in this respect, beats Macheath, as they used to say, " out of all cry;" but then the Captain, compared with Punch, is only a " petty-larceny villain," who is obliged to dose himself with brandy. Punch's confidence and presence of mind never desert him; and these qualities, combined with his personal but prudent courage, carry him through every difficulty, and enable him to triumph over every adversary. The great French satirist severely lashes those writers, who " make vice amiable."[*] and of this charge, we cannot acquit the author or authors of " Punch and Judy." In the person of the hero, and in the success of his criminal attempts, vice is most assuredly rendered too attractive, if we suppose that his example can have any effect upon those who witness his amusing performances.

Such is the character of Punch, as he is represented in this country, but in Italy he still preserves most of the qualities for which he was originally notorious. Baretti tells us, that his part is that of a " timid weak fellow, who is always thrashed by the other actors, and always boasts of victory after they are gone;"[†] and the author of a modern work, upon the manners and amusements of the Italians, thus speaks of the exhibitions in which Punch is engaged and of the figure he cuts in them.

" Two inferior theatres, La Fenice and San Carlino, both in the Largo del Castello, are chiefly devoted to farces and pantomimes. There you see Policinella in his genuine colours. Policinella is represented as a servant of Acerra,[‡] a village in the neighbourhood of Naples, and he is so highly gifted by nature and accomplished by education, that he is at once a thief, a liar, a coward, a braggart, and a debauchee: still the facetious way in

---

[*] Je ne puis estimer ces dangereux auteurs
    Qui, de l'honneur en vers infames déserteurs,
    Trahissent la vertu sur un papier coupable,
    Aux yeux de leurs lecteurs rendent le vice amiable.
                    " Boileau Art. Poet." chap. 4.

[†] Tolondron, p. 324.

[‡] See chap. I. of this work.

which he relates his various feats, enraptures the grovel-
ling countrymen.   He delights in licentious " double
entendre," gross jokes, and dirty tricks ; there is not a
single good quality in him : his cunning is very low, and
he is always outwitted when he meets with any person of
sense, so that in the end he is generally discovered, im-
prisoned, whipped, and hanged.   Such is the celebrated
Policinella.   There are many houses for puppet-shows,
where, at any time of the day, one may go in for a few
" grains," provided one's olfactory nerves are not too
keen for the smell produced by the crowd of dirty fellows
who resort to them.   There are also ambulatory puppet-
shows in the streets."*

It has been said, that " in England every thing intellectual advances by rapid strides;" and no more striking
or convincing proof can be given of its truth than the
change, especially of late years, which has occured in the
character of Punch.   In Italy, he has remained stationary:
he is there now, what he was two hundred years ago ; but
here, he is no longer the blunt-headed booby, " always
outwitted," represented in the preceding extract, but a
personage in general far too clever for any of those with
whom he has to deal : instead of being " discovered" and
" hanged," he contrives to have his executioner, " trussed
up" in his place ; and finally, by the happy union of
intellect and corporeal strength, defeats and destroys
" man's greatest enemy," and becomes " the devil's but-
cher," when the fiend hoped to have had him " in fee-
simple, with fine and recovery."

We cannot close the character of our hero without
inserting a sonnet (and its *coda*, as the Italians call it,)
in praise of Punch, by no less a man, if we are rightly

---

* " Italy, and the Italians in the Nineteenth Century,"
chap. 1.   The dress worn by Punch is represented in one of
Panelli's " Cinquanta Costumi Pittoreschi," Rome, 1816.   It
represents the performance of a puppet-show in the streets of
Rome, exactly in the same way as they are exhibited in this
country.   In Naples, sometimes a third person stands on an
elevation at the side, and explains, or " interprets," for the
characters.   Penelli makes Punch wear a black mask, like
Harlequin.

informed, than the poet, among whose latest works it was
to continue and vary the story of " Don Juan." It is
highly characteristic of the author, and of the representation
it celebrates with so much truth and vivacity.

SONNET TO PUNCH.

Triumphant Punch! with joy I follow thee
  Through the glad progress of thy wanton course;
  Where life is painful with such truth and force,
Its equal on our stage we never see,
Whether thou kill'st thy wife with jolly glee,
  Hurl'st thy sweet babe away without remorse,
  Mount'st, and art quickly thrown from off thy horse,
Or dance with " pretty Poll," so fair and free;
  Having first slain with just disdain her sire,
  Deaf to music of thy sheep-bell lyre :
Who loves not music, is not fit to live !
  Then, when the hangman comes, who can refuse
  To laugh, when thou his head into the noose
Hast nimbly thrust, while he gets no reprieve?
              Who feigns to grieve
Thou goest unpunish'd in the fiend's despite,
And slay'st him too, is but a hypocrite.
                  'Tis such delight
To see thee cudgel his black carcase antique,
For very rapture I am almost frantic !

Having now traced the history of Mr. Punch,* we shall
proceed, we believe, for the first time in this or any other
country, to put his performances upon record. It is time
to do so for the benefit of posterity ; lest, as society
gradually acquires a more superfine polish that it even now

---

* In reference to the origin of his family name, we may add,
that some have erroneously derived it from the liquor *punch*,
(which itself comes from the Indian *Palepuntz*, or *Palepunsche*,)
on the same principle that the Italian character Macaroni is
said to have been taken from the approved dish of that name
and as our Jack Pudding and the German *Hanns Wurst*, (before
mentioned,) from the attachment of the mob to puddings or
sausages. The fact is, that *Punch* is only a familiar abbreviation
of *Punchinello*, which is itself corrupted from *Pulcinella*.

possesses, it should be impossible, hereafter, to print what is fortunately yet considered innocent and harmless. Addison tell us, that " the merry people of the world are the amiable," and in the language of " a man forbid," we address ourselves to those,

> " Chi amano, senza smorfia e ipocrisia,
> " Gl' innocenti piaceri e l' allegria."

THE

TRAGICAL COMEDY, OR COMICAL TRAGEDY

OF

PUNCH AND JUDY.

PREFACE.

The following drama is founded chiefly upon the performance of an old Italian way-faring puppet-showman
of the name of Piccini, who has perambulated town and
country for the last forty or fifty years. Like the representations of our early stage, it was not by him distinguished into acts and scenes, but the divisions were easily
made; and the whole now assumes a shape, in which it
may rival most of the theatrical productions of the present
era, whether by Poole, popular for his "Paul Pry,"
Peake for his puns, Planché for his poetry, Peacock for
his parodies, or Payne for his plagiarisms.

Piccini lives in the classical vicinity of Drury Lane,
and is now infirm; but he still travels about, considering
it "no sin to labour in his vocation:" he is thus described
by a writer in a discontinued periodical, called the
"Literary Speculum," which we quote, because it is the
only printed notice we have seen of an individual so
generally known. It is to be observed, that the article
to which we are indebted, was published many years ago,
and the author of it speaks of his own youth, when
Piccini's age was "as a lusty winter, frosty but kindly,"
and before "time, the old clock-setter," had nearly let
him run the whole length of his chain without winding
him up again." "He (Piccini) was an Italian; a little
thick-set man, with a red humourous looking countenance.
He had lost one eye, but the other made up for the absence
of its fellow by a shrewdness of expression sufficient for
both. He always wore an oil-skin hat and a rough great
coat. At his back he carried a deal box, containing the
dramatis personæ of his little theatre; and in his hand
the trumpet, at whose glad summons, hundreds of merry
laughter-loving faces flocked round him with gaping

mouths and anxious looks, all eager to renew their acquaintance with their old friend and favourite, Punch. The theatre itself was carried by a tall man, who seemed a sort of sleeping partner in the concern, or mere *dumb waiter* on the other's operations." The woodcut on our title page, precisely corresponds with this lively description, making some allowance for the difference of age in the master of the puppet-show; still, however, not too old to carry his deal box and to blow an " inspiring air."

Besides Piccini's representation, we have compared the following pages with, and corrected them by the exhibitions of other perambulatory *artistes* (as our neighbours term them) now flourishing. It will be remarked that various parodies and snatches of songs are introduced, which are at present commonly omitted, though adding greatly to the humour and spirit of the piece : for many of these we are indebted to a manuscript, with the use of which we have been favoured, by a gentleman who undertook about the year 1796 to perform the task we have now executed, by giving the unwritten, if not strictly *extempore*, dialogue of " Punch and Judy" a permanent and tangible shape. The tunes and words for these musical accompaniments of the puppet-show have varied from time to time, according to circumstances; they take a tolerable extensive range, the oldest being adapted from " The Beggar's Opera," first acted January 29th, 1728, and the more modern from recent popular operas.

Piccini's exhibition was, in the first instance, purely Italian, and such colloquies as he introduced were in the language of that country : he soon learnt a little broken English, and adapted his show more to the taste of English audiences. It is too much to suppose that the notion that Punch is a foreigner, and ought always to speak like one, is taken from Piccini, because Punch has been looked upon as a stranger more welcome than most, from the first moment he set his foot in this country. The performers of " Punch and Judy," who are natives of Great Britain, generally endeavour to imitate an "outlandish dialect."

There is one peculiarity about Piccini's puppets which deserves notice : they are much better carved, the features having a more marked and comic expression than those of his rivals. He brought most of them over with him from Italy, and he complained that in England he had not been able to find any workmen capable of adequately supplying the loss, if by chance one of his figures had been broken or stolen. Why his Punch was made to squint, or at least to have what is known by the epithet of a swivel-eye, unless for the sake of humour or distinction, does not appear : in this obliquity of vision, he only follows the greatest hero of Italian romance, Orlando, of whom Pulci tell us,

> " Orlando molto ne gli occhi era fiero ;
> Tanto che alcun autore dice e pone,
> Ch' egli era un poco guercio, a dire il vero."

These lines are in Canto 20 of the " Morgante Maggiore, in the following Canto he repeats the assertion, in which he is supported by Boiardo in various parts of his " Orlando Innamorato," but particularly in Canto 41, where Astolpho in high indignation against the Paladin, exclaims,

> " ——— Ov' è quel guercio traditore,
> Ch' ha tanto ardir di dir ch' io son buffone?"

In fact, Orlando, as drawn by these poets, had little but his strength and courage to make the ladies love him, and the Pagans fear him ; and in all respects he was far inferior to Punch.

We have already spoken of Le Sage and Piron, as writers of Puppet Plays, and we might have introduced many other distinguished authors who lived about the opening of the last century. It is well known how popular this species of entertainment was, and still is in Germany ; and its dignity will receive a considerable accession, from the fact, that the greatest poet of that country, Goëthe, did not scruple to write one on the sacred story of Esther and Ahasuerus ; he calls it " Neueröffnetes moralisch-politisches Puppenspiel, and Hanns Wurst," or Jack Pudding, is employed to amuse the spectators between the acts.

DRAMATIS PERSONÆ.

PUNCH.	POLICE OFFICER.
SCARAMOUCH.	JACK KETCH.
THE CHILD.	THE DEVIL.
COURTIER.	TOBY.
DOCTOR.	HECTOR.
SERVANT.	
BLIND MAN.	JUDY.
CONSTABLE.	POLLY.

THE

TRAGICAL COMEDY, OR COMICAL TRAGEDY

OF

PUNCH AND JUDY.

Enter PUNCH—*after a few preliminary squeaks, he bows three times to the spectators ;—once in the centre, and once at each side of the stage, and then speaks the following*

Prologue.*

Ladies and Gentlemen, pray how you do ?
If you all happy, me all happy too.
Stop and hear my merry littel play ;
If me make you laugh, me need not make you pay.

Exit.

---

* The ancient *motions,* or puppet-shows, had prologues, as appears, among other authorities, from Jasper Mayne's "City Match," Act 5. Sc. 2.

——————" like a buskin'd prologue, in
A stately, high, majestic *motion* bare."

Powell also, as we have already seen, (*vide* Chap. 3) attacked Isaac Bickerstaff, Esq., in a prologue. Puppet-show men, now-a-days, seem to have adopted Cumberland's opinion, in his "Observer," that prologues and epilogues are useless appendages.

E

Act I.—Scene 1.

(PUNCH *is heard behind the scene, squeaking the tune of
"Malbroug s'en vat en guerre:"* he then makes his
appearance and dances about the stage, while he sings to
the same air,*)

Mr. Punch is one jolly good fellow,
His dress is all scarlet and yellow,†
And if now and then he gets mellow,
 It's only among his good friends.
 His money most freely he spends;
 To laugh and grow fat he intends;
With the girls he's a rogue and a rover;
He lives, while he can, upon clover
When he dies—it's only all over;
 And there Punch's comedy ends.
(*he continues to dance and sing, and then calls*
"Judy, my dear! Judy!")

Enter the DOG TOBY.

PUNCH. Hollo, Toby! who call'd you?. How you do,
Mr. Toby? Hope you very well, Mr. Toby.

TOBY. Bow, wow, wow!

PUNCH. How do my good friend, your master, Mr.
Toby? How do Mr. Scaramouch?‡

TOBY. Bow, wow, wow!

PUNCH. I'm glad to hear it. Poor Toby! What a
nice good-temper'd dog it is! No wonder his master is
so fond of him.

---

* This air and the Marseilles March, afterwards spoken of,
were doubtless first introduced, as substitutes for others which
had become less acceptable. Very recently the tune of Malbroug has again come into vogue with the lower orders.

† Scarlet and yellow are still proverbially called "Tom
Fool's colours," which may form another slight link of connection between Punch and the clown of our old comedies, and
the court jesters of our ancestors.

‡ The Italian character in the impromptu comedies, called
Scaramouch, was known in England, and considerably before

TOBY. *(snarls)* Arr! Arr!*

PUNCH. What! Toby! you cross this morning? You get out of bed the wrong way upwards?

TOBY. *(snarls again)* Arr! Arr!

PUNCH. Poor Toby. *(putting his hand out cautiously, and trying to coax the dog, who snaps at it)* Toby, you're one nasty cross dog : get away with you! *(strikes at him)*

TOBY. Bow, wow, wow! *(seizing PUNCH by the nose)*

PUNCH. Oh dear! Oh dear! My nose! my poor nose! my beautiful nose! Get away! get away, you nasty dog —I tell your master. Oh dear! dear!—Judy! Judy!

(PUNCH *shakes his nose, but cannot shake off the* DOG, *who follows him as he retreats round the stage. He continues to call* "Judy! Judy, my dear!" *until the* DOG *quits his hold, and exit)*

PUNCH. *(solus, and rubbing his nose with both hands)* Oh my nose! my pretty littel nose!† Judy! Judy! You nasty, nasty brute, I will tell you master of you. Mr. Scaramouch! *(calls)* My good friend, Mr. Scaramouch! Look what you nasty brute dog has done!

Pulcinello made his appearance. He gives the title to Ravencroft's comedy, and in D'Urfey's "Madam Fickle," licensed in 1676, Toby, the son of Mr. Tilbury, is made to employ it as a fashionable term of abuse, "Scaramouchi, Rascal, Poltron, Popinjay!—Son of twenty fathers!" &c. Act 2. Soon after the year 1720, Punch became a common character in afterpieces. In the "Weekly Journal" of Dec. 14, 1723, the plot of "Harlequin and Dr. Faustus" is given, in which it appears that Punch performed the part of one of the Doctor's Scholars. Duplessis was a celebrated Punch, and performed for Chetwood's benefit, in 1726.

* In reference to this sound, Shakspeare tells us that "R is the dog's letter. "Romeo and Juliet." Act 2. Scene 5.

† Punch's nose, which he here calls "little," ironically, according to the authority of one of our old play-wrights, would lead us to conclude him rather of Florentine than of Neapolitan origin.—Lodowick Barry, in his laughable comedy of manners, called "Ram Alley," printed in 1611, and reprinted in the last edition of "Dodsley's Old Plays," vol. 5. has a curious and humorous passage on the diversity of noses, a part

Enter SCARAMOUCH, *with a stick.*

SCARA. Hollo, Mr. Punch! what have you been doing to my poor dog?

PUNCH. (*retreating behind the side scene, on observing the stick, and peeping round the corner*) Ha! my good friend, how you do? glad to see you look so well. (*aside*) I wish you were farther with your nasty great stick.

SCARA. You have been beating and ill-using my poor dog, Mr. Punch.

PUNCH. He has been biting and ill-using my poor nose, —what have got there, sir?

SCARA. Where?

PUNCH. In your hand?

SCARA. A fiddle.

PUNCH. A fiddel! what a pretty thing is a fiddel!—can you play upon that fiddel?

SCARA. Come here, and I'll try.

PUNCH. No, thank you—I can hear the music here, very well.

SCARA. Then you shall try yourself. Can you play?

---

of which only is here applicable, but we shall be pardoned for quoting the whole.

————" I'll tell thee what,
A witty woman may with ease distinguish
All men by their noses, as thus : your nos
Tuscan is lovely, large, and broad,
Much like a goose; your valiant generous nose,
A crooked, smooth, and a great puffing nose.
Your scholar's nose is very fresh and raw,
For want of fire in winter, and quickly smells
His chops of mutton in his dish of porage.
Your puritan nose is very sharp and long,
And much like your widow's, and with ease can smell
An edifying capon five streets off."

This dissertation is worthy of Slaukenbergius. The nose of our hero is " lovely, large and broad," like " your nose Tuscan," and it is at the same time a

" valiant generous nose,
A crooked, smooth, and a great puffing nose."

PUNCH. (*coming in*) I do not know, 'till I try.* Let me see! (*takes the stick, and moves slowly about, singing the tune of the "Marche des Marseillois." He hits* SCARAMOUCH *a slight blow on his high cap, as if by accident*)

SCARA. You play very well, Mr. Punch; now let me try. I will give you a lesson how to play the fiddle. (*takes the stick, and dances to the same tune, hitting* PUNCH *a hard blow on the back of his head*) There's sweet music for you.

PUNCH. I no like you playing so well as my own. Let me again. (*takes the stick, and dances as before: in the course of his dance he gets behind* SCARAMOUCH, *and, with a violent blow knocks his head clean off his shoulders*) How you like that tune, my good friend? That sweet music, or sour music, eh? † He, he, he! (*laughing, and throwing away the stick*) You'll never hear such another tune, so long as you live, my boy. (*sings the tune of " Malbroug," and dances to it*) Judy, Judy, my dear! Judy, can't you answer, my dear?

JUDY. (*within*) Well! what do you want, Mr. Punch?

PUNCH. Come up stairs : I want you.

JUDY. Then want must be your master. I'm busy.

PUNCH. (*singing tune, " Malbroug"*)

Her answer genteel is and civil!
No wonder, you think, if we live ill,
And I wish her sometimes at the Devil,
   Since that's all the answer I get.
   Yet, why should I grumble and fret,
Because she's sometimes in a pet?

---

* This is a regular " Joe, page 47." Every body must remember Mr. Miller's story of the countryman, who was asked if he could play upon the violin, and who answered that he " did not know, because, as how, he had never tried." There may, however, be some corresponding joke in Italian. We have read it in French.

† " How sour sweet music is, when *time* is broke."
                       " Richard II." Act 5, Sc. 5.

Substitute *head* for *time*, and the line would be very applicable. Had Punch meant any allusion to it, he would have made the quotation and the change.

Though I really am sorry to say, sirs,
That that is too often her way, sirs.
For this, by and by, she shall pay, sirs.
  Oh, wives are an obstinate set!

Judy, my dear! (*calling*) Judy, my love—pretty Judy,
come up stairs.

Enter JUDY.

JUDY. Well, here I am! what do you want, now I'm
come?

PUNCH. (*aside*) What a pretty creature! An't she one
beauty?

JUDY. What do you want, I say?

PUNCH. A kiss! a pretty kiss! *(kisses her, while she
hits him a slap on the face)*

JUDY. Take that then: how do you like my kisses?
Will you have another?

PUNCH. No; one at a time, one at a time, my sweet
pretty wife. *(aside)* She always is so playful. Where's
the child? Fetch me the child, Judy, my dear.

Exit JUDY.

PUNCH. *(solus)* There's one wife for you! What a
precious darling creature? She go to fetch our child.*

---

* The MS. to which we are very much indebted for the
musical department of our drama, supplies another stanza to
the tune of " Malbroug," which we have excluded from the text,
as it contains already two specimens of the kind, and the simile
regarding her voice is used afterwards. It is, however, worth
adding in a note. Punch sings it after he has received the slap
on the face, and while Judy is gone for the child:

My wife is a beautiful darling,
And though her tongue goes like a starling,
We seldom have fighting or snarling.
  Her voice is delightful to hear!
  But take care you don't get too near;
  Sometimes her behaviour is queer:
With her hands she has always been handy.
I must doctor my face with some brandy,
And sweetened with white sugar-candy,
  I'll take it inside, never fear.

g.6k

Re-enter JUDY *with the* CHILD.

JUDY. Here's the child. Pretty dear! It knows its papa. Take the child.

PUNCH. (*holding out his hands*) Give it me—pretty littel thing! How like its sweet mamma!

JUDY. How awkward you are!

PUNCH. Give it me: I know how to nurse it so well as you do. (*she gives it him*) Get away! (*Exit* JUDY. PUNCH *nursing the* CHILD *in his arms*) What a pretty baby it is! was it sleepy then? Hush-a-by, by, by. (*sings to the tune of* "*Rest thee, Babe*")*

> Oh, rest thee, my baby,
> Thy daddy is here :
> Thy mammy's a gaby,
> And that's very clear.

> Oh, rest thee, my darling,
> Thy mother will come,
> With a voice like a starling ;—
> I wish she was dumb!

Poor dear littel thing! it cannot get to sleep: by, by; by, by, hush-a-by. Well, then, it shan't. (*dances the* CHILD, *and then sets it on his lap, between his knees, and sings the common nursery ditty,*)

> Dancy baby diddy ;
> What shall daddy do widdy?
> Sit on his lap,
> Give it some pap;
> Dancy, baby, diddy.†

---

* Evidently an interpolation since "Guy Mannering" was brought upon the stage. For what song this parody was substituted, cannot now be ascertained.

† The admirers of "the antiquities of nursery literature," (to use the words of the "Quarterly Review," which wisely devoted some sheets to the subject,) may like to see a different version of this "delicate and simple ditty," which we have on the highest authority. It runs thus:

> "Dancy, baby, dancy,
> How it shall gallop and prancy!
> Sit on my knee;
> Now kissy me:
> Dancy, baby, dancy."

(*after nursing it upon his lap,* PUNCH *sticks the* CHILD
*against the side of the stage, on the platform, and going
himself to the opposite side, runs up to it, clapping his
hands, and crying* " Catchee, catchee, catchee !" *He
then takes it up again, and it begins to cry*)
What is the matter with it. Poor thing ! It has got
the stomach ache, I dare say. *(child cries)* Hush-a-by,
hush-a-by ! *(sitting down, and rolling it on his knees)*
Naughty child !—Judy ! *(calling)* the child has got the
stomach ache. Pheu ! Nasty child ! Judy, I say ! (CHILD
continues to cry) Keep quiet, can't you ? (*hits it a box on*
the ear) Oh you filthy child ! What have you done ? I
won't keep such a nasty child. Hold your tongue ! (*strikes
the* CHILD's *head several times against the side of the stage*)
There !—there ! there ! How you like that ? I thought
I stop your squalling. Get along with you, nasty, naughty,
crying child. (*throws it over the front of the stage, among
the spectators*)—He ! he ! he ! (*laughing and singing to the
same tune as before*)

Get away, nasty baby ;
There it goes over
Thy mammy's a gaby,
Thy daddy's a rover.

Re-enter JUDY.

JUDY. Where is the child ?
PUNCH. Gone—gone to sleep.*
JUDY. What have you done with the child, I say ?
PUNCH. Gone to sleep, I say.
JUDY. What have you done with it ?
PCNCH. What have I done with it ?
JUDY. Ay ; done with it !† I heard it crying just now.
Where is it ?

---

* Punch equivocates between death itself and the " ape of
death."
" After life's fitful fever it *sleeps* well."
" Macbeth," Act 3, Scene 2.
† Judy might say with the Moor—

Done with it ?—" By heaven, he echoes me,
As if there were some monster in his thought
Too hideous to be shewn."—" Othello," Act 3, Scene 3.

72^2

PUNCH. How should I know?

JUDY. I heard you make the pretty darling cry.

PUNCH. I dropped it out at window.

JUDY. Oh you cruel horrid wretch, to drop the pretty baby out at window. Oh! (*cries, and wipes her eyes with the corner of her white apron*) You barbarous man. Oh!

PUNCH. You shall have one other soon, Judy, my dear. More where that come from.*

JUDY. I'll make you pay for this, depend upon it.

Exit in haste.

PUNCH. There she goes. What a piece of work about nothing!†

(*dances about and sings, beating time with his head, as he turns round, on the front of the stage*)

Re-enter JUDY *with a stick; she comes in behind, and hits* PUNCH *a sounding blow on the back of the head, before he is aware.*

JUDY. I'll teach you to drop my child out at window.

PUNCH. So—o—oftly, Judy, so—o—oftly! (*rubbing*

---

* This may remind the reader of an anecdote in Machiavelli's "Discorsi" (Lib. 3, cap. 6, Delle Congiurie), where Caterina the wife of Girolamo Riorio, Count of Forli, in a very extraordinary manner, defied her enemies, and shewed how little she valued the lives of her sons. Mr. Roscoe ("Life of Lorenzo de Medici," 2, 164, edition 1825), does not seem to be aware that the story is to be found in Machiavelli, and he quotes Muratori's "Annals," 9, 556, for his authority. Muratori treats the point with great decorum;—"Rispose loro quella forte femmina che se avessero fatti perir que' figliuoli, restavano a lei le forme per farne de gli altri."

† "This nothing's more than matter," and yet Punch was right in the sense in which Shakespeare speaks in "Coriolanus;"—

"It was a thing of nothing—*titleless*,"

for the infant has no name, and it is uncertain whether it ever was christened. We have heard it invariably spoken of as "the child;" and even its sex is doubtful, unless we take the word of Thomson,—"Heroes are sires of boys,"—and then we shall, of course, conclude that Punch's offspring was a man-child.

the back of his head with his hand) Don't be a fool now.*
What you at?

Judy. What! you'll drop my poor baby out at window
again, will you? (*hitting him continually on the head*)

Punch. No, I never will again. (*she still hits him*)
Softly, I say, softly. A joke's a joke.

Judy. Oh, you nasty cruel brute! (*hitting him again*)
I'll teach yon.

Punch. But me no like such teaching. What! you're
in earnest are you?

Judy. Yes, (*hit*) I (*hit*) am. (*hit*)

Punch. I'm glad of it: me no like such jokes.† (*she
hits him again*) Leave off, I say. What! you won't,
won't you?

---

* This was the great Grimaldi's celebrated exclamation in
" Mother Goose" and elsewhere, and from him it seems borrowed : we call him " the great Grimaldi" to distinguish him
from his great grandfather, grandfather, father, and son, for
they have been a succession of clowns for five generations.
The most remarkable of " Joey's" predecessors was called
" Jambes de fer," from the strength and spring of his limbs : he
was the grandfather and a great favorite with the ladies—
" ferrum est quod amant :" he once broke a chandelier by lofty
vaulting, and with a piece of the glass almost knocked out the
eye of the Turkish Ambassador, who made it a formal com-
plaint to the French Court. " Joey's" son promised much, and
cannot be said to have *performed* little ; for all the winter he was
at Covent-Garden, and all the summer at Sadler's Wells ; however, he never reached a point of comparison with his father ;

" Compared with whom all other clowns were fools."

† This is a jest in almost every language, but it is particularly common in Italy. It is inserted in Domenichi's Collection of " Motti Burle e Facetie :" Venice, 1565. It is of a
piece with the story relating to General ——, whom T. H.
kicked in a ball-room. " What do you mean by that, sir?"
(cried the General,) " Am I to take that as a personal affront?"
—" To be sure you are," replied T. H.—" I am glad of it,
(returned the General,) I like people to speak intelligibly—it
saves the trouble of farther *explanation.*" Accordingly, T. H.
heard no more from the officer ; who afterwards got so often
affronted, and received patiently so many insults, that he
acquired the nick-name of " the *receiver* General."

JUDY. No, I won't. (*hits him*)

PUNCH. Very well: then now come my turn to teach you. (*he snatches at, and struggles with her for the stick, which he wrenches from her, and strikes her with it on the head, while she runs about to different parts of the stage to get out of his way*) How you like my teaching, Judy, my pretty dear? (*hitting her*)

JUDY. O pray, Mr. Punch—no more!

PUNCH. Yes, one littel more lesson. (*hits her again*) There, there, there! (*she falls down, with her head over the platform of the stage; and as he continues to hit at her, she puts up her hand to guard her head*) Any more.

JUDY. No, no, no more. (*lifting up her head*)

PUNCH. (*knocking down her head*) I thought I should soon make you quiet.

JUDY. (*again raising her head*) No.

PUNCH. (*again knocking it down, and following up his blows until she is lifeless*) Now if you're satisfied, I am. (*perceiving that she does not move*) There, get up, Judy my dear; I won't hit you any more. None of your sham-Abram.* This is only your fun. You got the head-ache? Why, you only asleep. Get up, I say! Well then, get down. (*tosses the body down with the end of his stick*) He, he, he! (*laughing*) To lose a wife is to get a fortune.†

---

* This is a very old English word; not, however, inserted and explained by the Rev. H. J. Todd. *Sham* is said to be derived from the Welch, and *Abram* is from what were formerly called "Abram," or Abraham men," who pretended to be poor and sick, and therefore objects of charity. (See "Dodsley's Old Plays," new edition, vol. 2, page 4, note 2.) To sham-Abram is a term in daily use:

"*Sham-Abram* you may
In any fair way,
But you must not sham Abraham Newland."
"T. Dibdin's Song."

Bank-notes were formerly signed " Abraham Newland."

† The English proverb is, " he that loses his wife and six-pence, loses a tester." It is put into the mouth of Sancho, in Act 2 of Durfey's " Don Quixote," Part 1.

" Who'd be plagued with a wife
    That could set himself free
With a rope or a knife,
    Or a good stick, like me.

(he throws away the body with his stick)

Enter PRETTY POLLY.†

PUNCH. (seeing her, and singing out of " The Beggar's Opera,"‡ while she dances)

When the heart of a man is oppress'd with cares,
The clouds are dispelled when a woman appears, &c.

PUNCH. (aside) What a beauty ! What a pretty creature !§

(extending his arms, and then clasping his hands in

---

* Evidently from Juvenal, Sat. 6.

" Ferre potes dominam salvis tot restibus ullam ?
    Cum pateant altæ caligantesque fenestræ,
    Cum tibi vicinum se prœbeat Æmilius pons ?

Here it seems doubtful whether the poet means to recommend the hen-pecked husband himself to use the halter, leap
out of the window, &c. or that he should hang his wife, or
give her the benefit of the air. Punch's actions supply a com-
mentary on his words, if any were wanting.

† Sometimes called Nancy, and hence the old saying,—

" For fun and fancy,
    As Punch kissed Nancy."

‡ This song was probably first introduced into a puppet-
show, at the time when Gay's work was so extravagantly
popular ; but not more popular than it deserved to be.
§ In this copy of " Punch and Judy," Pretty Polly is merely
a mute, which perhaps might recommend her to our hero, in
contrast with his late spouse. In a few of the representations
she speaks ; and one which was popular in 1795 and 1796, contained the following scene. We ought to premise, that in that
show, Polly was supposed to be the daughter of a gentleman
whom Punch had just slain, in a quarrel regarding his performances on the sheep-bell.

Enter POLLY very gaily dressed.

POLLY. Where is my father ? my dear father !

76

admiration. She continues to dance, and dances round him, while he surveys her in silent delight. He then begins to sing a slow tune and foots it with her; and, as the music quickens, they jig it backwards and forwards, and sideways, to all parts of the stage. At last, Punch catches the lady in his arms and kisses her most audibly, while she appears "nothing loth." After waltzing, they dance to the tune of " The White Cockade," and Punch sings as follows:)

I love you so, I love you so,
I never will leave you; no, no, no:
If I had all the wives of wise King Sol,
I would kill them all for my pretty Poll.

Exeunt dancing.

PUNCH. (*aside*) What a beauty!
POLLY. Who killed my poor father? Oh! Oh! (*cries*)
PUNCH. 'Twas I.
POLLY. Oh! Cruel wretch, why did you kill my father?
PUNCH. For your sake, my love.
POLLY. Oh, you barbarian!
PUNCH. Don't cry so, my dear. You will cry your pretty eyes out, and that would be a pity.
POLLY. Oh, oh! How could you kill him?
PUNCH. He would not let me have you, and so I killed him. If you take on so, I must cry too—Oh, oh! (*pretending to weep*) How sorry I am!
POLLY. And are you really sorry?
PUNCH. Yes, very sorry—look how I cry.
POLLY. (*aside*) What a handsome young man. It is a pity he should cry so.—How the tears run down his beautiful long nose!—Did you kill my father out of love of me, and are you sorry? If you are sorry, I must forgive you.
PUNCH. I could kill myself for love of you, much more your father.
POLLY. Do you then really love me?
PUNCH. I do! I do!
POLLY. Then I most love you!"
Then they embrace, kiss, and dance. The whole scene, barring the dancing, seems modelled upon the interview between Richard III. and Lady Anne. It is copied from the MS. we have before mentioned.

Act II.

Enter a Figure *dressed like a Courtier, who sings a slow air, and moves to it with great gravity and solemnity. He first takes off his hat on the right of the theatre, and then on the left, and carries it in his hand. He then stops in the centre; the music ceases, and suddenly his throat begins to elongate, and his head gradually rises until his neck is taller than all the rest of his body. After pausing for some time, the head sinks again; and, as soon as it has descended to its natural place, the* Figure *exits.**

Enter Punch *from behind the curtain, where he had been watching the manœuvres of the Figure.*

Punch. Who the devil are you, me should like to know, with your long neck? You may get it stretched for you, one of these days, by somebody else.† It's a very fine day. *(peeping out, and looking up at the sky)* I'll go fetch my horse, and take a ride to visit my pretty Poll. *(he sings to the tune of* " Sally in our Alley")

Of all the girls that are so smart,
There's none like pretty Polly :
She's the darling of my heart,
She is so plump and jolly.

Exit, singing.

---

* This scene is peculiar to Piccini, and he defies all the other exhibitors of Puppet-shows in England to make the figure take off the hat with one hand. This is the true reason for its introduction; and it is not easy to see in what way it relates to Mr. Punch and his adventures, unless, as he is now in the midst of his career of vice and crime, the stretching of the neck is to be taken as an awful forewarning of the danger of the same kind the hero is likely to incur under the hands of Jack Ketch.

" You have done well,
That men must lay their murders on your neck."

is a passage in " Othello."—If it be meant that Punch should lay his murders on the *neck* of this mysterious personage, it is clear that there is room enough for all of them.

† " I pr'ythee keep that for the hangman."—" Henry IV. Part I." And Punch might add, as the forewarner appears to

I

78

Re-enter PUNCH, *leading his Horse by the bridle over his arm. It prances about, and seems very unruly.*

PUNCH. Wo, ho! my fine fellow, Wo, ho! Hector.* Stand still, can't you, and let me get my foot up to the stirrup.

> (*while* PUNCH *is trying to mount, the horse runs away round the stage, and* PUNCH *sets off after him, catches him by the tail, and so stops him.* PUNCH *then mounts, by sitting on the front of the stage, and with both his hands lifting one of his legs over the animal's back. At first, it goes pretty steadily, but soon quickens its pace; while* PUNCH, *who does not keep his seat very well, cries,* " Wo, ho, Hector! wo, ho!" *but to no purpose, for the horse sets off at full gallop, jerking* PUNCH *at every stride with great violence.* PUNCH *lays hold round the neck, but is ultimately thrown upon the platform*)†

---

be a courtier, "I know thou worship'st as St. Nicholas truly as a man of falsehood may."

* The horses of the ancient heroes of romance, especially in Italy, (the birth-place of our hero,) had all their names, sometimes descriptive of their qualifications, or of peculiar marks, or ornaments: that of Orlando, as everybody knows, was Baiardo ; that of Aglante, Rabicano, and that of the Cid, Babieca, &c. For this reason, too, Don Quixote gives his steed the style and title of Rozinante, " as it was not fit that so famous a knight's horse, and chiefly being so good a beast, should want a known name."—" Shelton's Don Quixotte," Edition 1652, fol. 2.

† Punch is no great horseman, but it is to be remembered that he was not a gentleman born or bred ; and, as Spenser says,

> " But chiefly skill to ride seems a science
>   Proper to *gentle* blood."

Sir Philip Sidney opens his " Defence of Poesie" with an account of his industry at the Emperor's court in acquiring perfection in this art, which old Ascham, in his "Schoolmaster," praises very extravagantly, quoting the " three excellent praises amongst those noble gentlemen, the old Persians— always to speak truth, to ride fair, and shoot well."

PUNCH. Oh, dear! Oh, lord! Help! help! I am
murdered! I'm a dead man! Will nobody save my life?
Doctor! Doctor! Come, and bring me to life again. I'm
a dead man. Doctor! Doctor! Doctor!

Enter DOCTOR.

DOCTOR. Who calls so loud?*
PUNCH. Oh, dear! Oh, lord! murder!
DOCTOR. What is the matter? Bless me who is this?
My good friend, Mr. Punch? Have you had an accident,
or are you only taking a nap on the grass after dinner?
PUNCH. Oh, Doctor! Doctor! I have been thrown: I
have been killed.
DOCTOR. No, no, Mr. Punch; not so bad as that, sir:
you are not killed.
PUNCH. Not killed, but speechless.† Oh, Doctor!
Doctor!

---

* So the Apothecary, in " Romeo and Juliet," of whom we
say, as Dante does of the she-wolf—

"Che di tutte brame
Sembiava carca nella sua magrezza.

enters at the exclamation of the hero, with " Who calls so
loud?" Punch's Doctor is quite " another guess sort of a gentleman," to use a phrase of Farquhar's, " fat with full fees and
no physic."

† A good deal has been written on the etymology and mean-
ing of what is called an Irish *bull*, of which we have here a
specimen; some have supposed it to be derived from a ridicule
of the Pope's *bulls*, &c., &c.; but its origin is very simple: a
bull is a blunder; and only let the reader pronounce the two
first letters of the word *blunder*, and he immediately has the
true etymology—*blunder*, or per ellipsin *bl*. Milton correctly
defines a *bull*, when he says it " takes away the essence of that
which it calls itself." (*Smectymn. Apology.*) but rather before
the time when he flourished it seems to have been almost
synonymous, with a jest. Thus in Shirley's " Gamester," 1637,
Act 3, Hazard says to Wilding,

————" He will talk desperately
And swear he is the father of all the *bulls*
Since Adam : if all fail, he has a project
To print his *jests*.

DOCTOR. Where are you hurt? Is it here? (*touching his head*)

PUNCH. No; lower.

DOCTOR. Here? (*touching his breast*)

PUNCH. No; lower, lower.

DOCTOR. Here, then? (*going downwards*)

PUNCH. No; lower still.

DOCTOR. Then, is your handsome leg broken?

PUNCH. No; higher.

    (*as the* DOCTOR *leans over Punch's legs, to examine them,* PUNCH *kicks him in the eye*)

DOCTOR. Oh, my eye! my eye!   *Exit.*

PUNCH. (*solus*) Aye, you're right enough; it is my eye, and Betty Martin too.* (*jumping up, and dancing and singing—tune,* " Malbroug.")

    The Doctor is surely an ass, sirs,
    To think I'm as brittle as glass, sirs;
    But I only fell down on the grass, sirs,
    And my hurt—it is all my eye.

    (*while* PUNCH *is singing and dancing, the* DOCTOR *enters behind, with a stick, and hits* PUNCH *several times on the head;* PUNCH *shakes his ears.*)

PUNCH. Hollo! hollo! Doctor—what game you up to now? Have done! What you got there?

DOCTOR. Physic, Mr. Punch; (*hits him*) physic for your hurt.

PUNCH. Me no like physic; it give me one headache.

DOCTOR. That's because you do not take enough of it. (*hits him again*) The more you take, the more good it will do you. (*hits him*)

WILDING. His *bulls* you mean.

HAZARD. You're right,
    And dedicate 'em to the gamesters," &c.

  * This joke is much more proper, in some respects, in Catholic Italy, than in Protestant England, where we have left off praying to Saints. The saying is, however, as is well known, derived from times prior to the Reformation, when *Mihi, beate Martine* was the commencement of an address to St. Martin: the use of it, as an expression of ridicule, implying incredulity, must, of course, have been posterior to that event, when *disbelief* in the efficacy of such addresses became general.

F

PUNCH. So you doctors always say. Try how you like it yourself.

DOCTOR. We never take our own physic, if we can help it. (*hits him*) A little more, Mr. Punch, and you will soon be well.

> (*hits him ;—during this part of the dialogue, the* DOCTOR *hunts* PUNCH *to different parts of the stage, and at last gets him into a corner, and belabours him until* PUNCH *seems almost stunned*)

PUNCH. Oh, Doctor! Doctor! no more, no more! enough physic for me ; I am quite well now.

DOCTOR. Only another dose. (*hits him*)

PUNCH. No more!—turn and turn about is all fair, you know. (PUNCH *makes a desperate effort, closes with the* DOCTOR, *and after a struggle, succeeds in getting the stick from him*) Now, Doctor, your turn to be physicked. (*beating the* DOCTOR*)

DOCTOR. Hold, Mr. Punch; I don't want any physic, my good sir.

PUNCH. Oh, yes, you do; you very bad; you must take it; I the doctor now.† (*hits him*) How do you like physic? (*hits*) It will do you good. (*hits*) This will soon cure you: (*hits*) physic! (*hits*) physic! (*hits*) physic! (*hits*)

DOCTOR. Oh, pray, Mr. Punch, no more! one pill of that physic is a dose.

PUNCH. Doctors always die when they take their own physic. (*hits him*) Another small dose, and you never want physic again. (*hits him*) There, don't you feel the physic in your inside? (PUNCH *thrusts the end of the stick into the* DOCTOR's *stomach; the* DOCTOR *falls down dead, and* PUNCH, *as before, tosses away the body with the end of his staff*) He, he, he! (*laughing*) Now, Doctor, you may cure

---

* We cannot call Punch *lethargicus*, but, at all events
——————"fit pugil et medicum urget."
As one of our old translators has it,
     · " He knocks down the quack
        On the flat of his back."
† " He will be the physician that should be the patient."
         " Troilus and Cressida," Act 2.

82

yourself, if you can. (*sings and dances to the tune of* " Green grow the rushes, O."*)

> Right toll de riddle doll,
> There's an end of him, by goll!*
> I'll dance and sing
> Like any thing,
> With music for my pretty Poll.   *Exit.*

Enter PUNCH, *with a large sheep-bell, which he rings violently, and dances about the stage, shaking the bell and his head at the same time, and accompanying the music with his voice ;—tune, " Morgiana in Ireland."*

> Mr. Punch is a very gay man,
> He is the fellow the ladies for winning, oh ;
> Let them do whatever they can,
> They never can stand his talking and grinning, oh.

Enter a SERVANT, *in a foreign livery.*

SERVANT. Mr. Punch, my master, he say he no like dat noise.

PUNCH. (*with surprise and mocking him*) Your master, he say he no like dat noise ! What noise ?

SERVANT. Dat nasty noise.

PUNCH. Do you call music a noise.†

---

* A very respectable ancient English oath. *Goll*, in our old writers, and in the vulgar tongue, is the same as *hand;* so that to swear " goll," is nothing more than to swear by one's hand. " By goles," or " golls," is still used in the country. Thus, in S. Rowley's " Noble Soldier," 1634, Act 3. Baltazar says to Onelia, (a lady of Spanish and not of Irish extraction, as might be supposed by her name,) " Say'st thou me so ? Give me thy *goll*, thou art a noble girl," &c. We leave it to future sagacious commentators on this play, to shew that " learning is somewhere vain," and to multiply quotations on a point never disputed.

† Our less refined ancestors used to do so. "A noise of fiddlers," "a noise of flutes," &c., are common expressions in old plays of the reigns of Elizabeth and James I. Punch's ear for music resembles that of Nick Bottom. "I have a reasonable good ear for music : let us have the tongs and the bones."

SERVANT. My master he no lika de music, Mr. Punch, so he'll have no more noise near his house.*

PUNCH. He don't, don't he? Very well. (PUNCH *runs about the stage ringing his bell as loudly as he can*)

SERVANT. Get away, I say wid dat nasty bell.

PUNCH. What bell?

SERVANT. That bell. (*striking it with his hand*)

PUNCH. That's a good one. Do you call this a bell? (*patting it*) It is an organ.

SERVANT. I say it is a bell, a nasty bell. ·

PUNCH. I say it is an organ. (*striking him with it*) What you say it is now?

SERVANT. An organ, Mr. Punch.

PUNCH. An organ? I say it is a fiddle. Can't you see? (*offers to strike him again*)

SERVANT. It is a fiddle.

PUNCH. I say it is a drum.

SERVANT. It is a drum, Mr. Punch.

PUNCH. I say it is a trumpet.

SERVANT. Well, so it is a trumpet. But bell, organ, fiddle, drum, or trumpet, my master, he say he no lika de music.

PUNCH. Then bell, organ, fiddle, drum, or trumpet, Mr. Punch he say your master is a fool.

SERVANT. And he say too, he will not have it near his house.

PUNCH. He's a fool, I say, not to like my sweet music. Tell him so: be off. (*hits him with the bell*) Get along. (*driving the* SERVANT *round the stage, backwards, and*

---

* Part of a now unacted scene in " Othello," very much resembles this. The Clown enters, and complains of certain serenaders hired by Cassio, and tells them, "the General so likes your music, that he desires you of all loves to make no more noise with it.

1ST MUSICIAN. Well, sir, we will not.

CLOWN. If you have any music that may not be heard, to't again: but as they say, to hear music, the General does not greatly care.

1ST MUSICIAN. We have none such, sir.

CLOWN. Then put your pipes in your bag and hie away. Go—vanish into air! Away!"

84²

striking him often with the bell) Be off, be off. (*knocking
him off the stage. Exit* SERVANT. PUNCH *continues to
ring the bell as loudly as before, while he sings and dances*)

Re-enter SERVANT, *slily, with a stick.*

(PUNCH *perceiving him, retreats behind the side curtain, and remains upon the watch. The* SERVANT
does the same, but leaves the end of the stick visible.
PUNCH *again comes forward, sets down his bell
very gently, and creeps across the stage, (marking
his steps with his hands upon the platform, to
ascertain whereabouts his enemy is. He then
returns to his bell, takes it up, and, going quietly
over the stage, hits the* SERVANT *a heavy blow
through the curtain, and exit, ringing his bell on
the opposite side*)

SERVANT. You one nasty, noisy, impudent blackguard,
Me catch you yet. (*hides again as before*)

(*enter* PUNCH, *and strikes him as before with the
bell. The* SERVANT *pops out, and aims a blow,
but not quickly enough to hit* PUNCH, *who exit*)

SERVANT. You dirty scoundrel, rascal, thief, vagabond,
blackguard, and liar, you shall pay for this, depend upon it.

(*he stands back. Enter* PUNCH, *with his bell, who
seeing the* SERVANT *with his stick, retreats instantly,
and returns, also armed with a bludgeon, which he
does not at first shew. The* SERVANT *comes forward, and strikes* PUNCH *on the head so hard a
blow, that it seems to confuse him*)

SERVANT. Me teach you how to ring your nasty noisy
bell near de gentil-mens houses.

PUNCH. (*recovering*) Two can play at that. (*hits the
SERVANT with his stick. A conflict:—after a long struggle,
during which the combatants exchange staves, and perform
various manœuvres, PUNCH gains the victory, and knocks
his antagonist down on the platform, by repeated blows on
the head*)

SERVANT. Oh, dear! Oh, my head!

PUNCH. And oh, your tail, too. (*hitting him there*) How
do you like that, and that, and that? (*hitting him each
time*) Do you like that music better than the other?—

This is my bell, *(hits)* this my organ, *(hits)* this my fiddle, *(hits)* this my drum, *(hits)* and this my trumpet, *(hits)* there! a whole concert for you.

SERVANT. No more! me dead.

PUNCH. Quite dead.

SERVANT. Yes, quite.

PUNCH. Then there's the last for luck. *(hits him and kills him. He then takes hold of the body by its legs, swings it round two or three times, and throws it away)*

ACT III.

Enter an OLD BLIND MAN, *feeling his way with a staff; he goes to the opposite side when he knocks.*

BLIND MAN. Poor blind man, Mr. Punch; I hope you'll bestow your charity; I hear that you are very good and kind to the poor, Mr. Punch; pray have pity upon me, and may you never know the loss of your tender eyes! *(listens, putting his ear to the side, and hearing nobody coming, knocks again)* I lost my sight by the sands in Egypt;* poor blind man. Pray, Mr. Punch, have compassion upon the poor stone blind. *(coughs, and spits over the side)* Only a halfpenny to buy something for my bad cough. Only one halfpenny. *(knocks again)*

Enter PUNCH, *and receives one of the knocks, intended for the door, upon his head.*

PUNCH. Hollo! you old blind blackguard, can't you see?

BLIND MAN. No, Mr. Punch. Pray, sir, bestow your charity upon a poor blind man, with a bad cough. *(coughs)*

PUNCH. Get along, get along; don't trouble me :— nothing for you.

BLIND MAN. Only a halfpenny! Oh, dear! my cough is so bad! *(coughs and spits in* PUNCH'S *face)*

---

* Of cause, this explanation of the cause of blindness was inserted after Sir Ralph Abercrombie's expedition to Egypt, when many beggars were seen about the streets asking alms on the same score. Before that date, some other popular cause was, no doubt, assigned.

PUNCH. Hollo! Was my face the dirtiest place you could find to spit in?* Get away! you nasty old blackgard! Get away! (*seizes the* BLIND MAN'S *staff, and knocks him off the stage.*—PUNCH *hums a tune, and dances to it; and then begins to sing, in the mock Italian style, the following words, pretending to play the fiddle on his arm, with the stick*)

When I think on you, my jewel,†
    Wonder not my heart is sad;
You're so fair, and yet so cruel,
    You're enough to drive me mad.

On thy lover take some pity:
    And relieve his bitter smart.
Think you Heaven has made you pretty,
    But to break your lover's heart?

Enter a CONSTABLE.

CONSTABLE. Leave off your singing, Mr. Punch, for I'm come to make you sing on the wrong side of your mouth.

PUNCH. Why, who the devil are you?

CONSTABLE. Don't you know me?

PUNCH. No, and don't want to know you.

CONSTABLE. Oh, but you must: I am the constable.

PUNCH. And who sent for you?

CONSTABLE. I am sent for you.

PUNCH. I don't want constable. I can settle my own business without constable, I thank you. I don't want constable.

CONSTABLE. But the constable wants you.

---

* This joke is of Italian origin. Bandello (Part 3, Novel 42) makes the Spanish Ambassador spit in the face of one of the servants of the famous Roman courtezan Imperia, whose house was most splendidly furnished. It is, however, older than Bandello's time; and it is also found in the Italian jest book, before quoted, collected by Domenichi in 1565.

† A real Italian air and song, introduced by Piccini, of which this is a translation: the first words of the original are—
    " Quando pens' io à la mia bella."

Punch. The Devil he does! What for, pray?

Constable. You killed Mr. Scaramouch. You knocked his head off his shoulders.

Punch. What's that to you? If you stay here much longer, I'll serve you the same.

Constable. Don't tell me. You have committed murder, and I've a warrant for you.

Punch. And I've a, warrant for you. (Punch *knocks him down, and dances and sings about the stage, to the tune of* " Green grow the Rushes O.")

Enter an Officer, *in a cocked hat with a cockade, and a long pigtail.**

Officer. Stop your noise, my fine fellow

Punch. Shan't.

Officer. I'm an officer.

Punch. Very well. Did I say you were not?

Officer. You must go with me. You killed your wife and child.

Punch. They were my own, I suppose; and I had a right to do what I liked with them.

Officer. We shall see that, I'm come to take you up.

Punch. And I'm come to take you down. (Punch *knocks him down, and sings and dances as before)*

Enter Jack Ketch, *in a fur-cap.* Punch, *while dancing, runs up against him without seeing him.*

Punch. *(with some symptoms of alarm)* My dear Sir,— I beg you one thousand pardons : very sorry.

J. Ketch. Aye, you'll be sorry enough before I've done with you. Don't you know me?

Punch. Oh, sir, I know you very well, and I hope you very well, and Mrs. Ketch very well.

J. Ketch. Mr. Punch, you're a very bad man. Why did you kill the Doctor?

Punch. In self defence.

J. Ketch. That won't do.

---

* The ordinary performers of puppet-shows do not seem clearly to understand the distinction between an officer of the army and an officer of the police.

PUNCH. He wanted to kill me.

J. KETCH. How?

PUNCH. With his d——d physic.

J. KETCH. That's all gammon. You must come to prison : my name's Ketch.

PUNCH. *Ketch* that then. (PUNCH *knocks down* JACK KETCH, *and continues to dance and sing**)

Enter behind, one after the other, the CONSTABLE, *the* OFFICER, *and* JACK KETCH. *They fall upon* PUNCH *in the order in which they enter, and after a noisy struggle, they pin him in a corner, and finally carry him off, while he lustily calls out "* Help ! murder !*" &c.*

SCENE II.

(the curtain rises at the back of the stage rises, and discovers PUNCH *in prison, rubbing his nose against the bars and poking it through them)*

PUNCH. Oh dear ! Oh dear ! what will become of poor pill-garlick now. My pretty Poll, when shall I see you again ? (*sings to the air of* " Water parted from the Sea")

> Punch, when parted from his dear,
> Still must sing in doleful tune.
> I wish I had those rascals here,
> I'd settle all their hashes soon !

---

* After the defeat of Jack Ketch, we have sometimes seen, with a total disregard of his rank and office, the Chief Justice of England introduced, for the purpose of making the caption of Punch. The dialogue between the two was equally *infra dignitatem*, at least on the part of the first Judge of the land.

CHIEF JUSTICE. Hollo ! Punch, my boy !

PUNCH. Hollo ! who are you with your head like a cauliflower ?

CHIEF JUSTICE. Don't you know me ? I'm the Lord Chief Justice.

PUNCH. I don't care if you're the Lord Chancellor. You shan't get me into Chancery, that's all.

CHIEF JUSTICE. But I shall get you into prison.—You're a murderer ! you've killed I don't know how many people.

Enter JACK KETCH. *He fixes a gibbet on the platform of the stage, and exit.*

PUNCH. Well, I declare now, that very pretty! That must be a gardener. What a handsome *three* he has planted just opposite the window, for a prospect!*

Enter the CONSTABLE. *He places a ladder against the gibbet, and exit.*

PUNCH. Stop thief! stop thief! There's one pretty rascal for you. He come back again and get up the ladder to steal the fruit out of the tree.

Enter two MEN *with a coffin. They set it down on the platform, and exeunt.*

PUNCH. What that for, I wonder? Oh dear, I see now: what one fool I was! That is large basket for the fruit be put into.

Re-enter JACK KETCH.

J. KETCH. Now, Mr. Punch, you may come out, if you like it.

PUNCH. Thank you, kindly; but me very well where I am. This very nice place, and pretty prospect.

J. KETCH. What, won't you come out, and have a good dinner for nothing?

PUNCH. Much obliged, Mr. Ketch, but I have had my dinner for nothing already.†

PUNCH. If you don't know, you had better go and learn.

CHIEF JUSTICE. That won't do, my fine fellow. You're a murderer, and you must come and be hanged.

PUNCH. I'll be hanged if I do. (*knocks down the Chief Justice, and dances and sings*)

* Of course Punch does not think what he says, but he only "plays with his fate;" as Racine remarks in "Athalie," (Act 2)

    "Les malheurs n'avoient pas abattu sa fierté,"
although in the commencement of this scene the recollection of his mistress had a little "rebated the edge of his hilarity."

† Among the "Rime burlesche di varj Autori," originally collected by Grazzini, is a very humorous *Capitolo*, in praise of debt, (attributed by some to Berni, and by the editor of

J. KETCH. Then a good supper?

PUNCH. I never eat suppers : they are not wholesome.

J. KETCH. But you must come out. Come out, and be hanged.*

PUNCH. You would not be so cruel.

J. KETCH. Why were you so cruel as to commit so many murders?

PUNCH. But that's no reason why you should be cruel, too, and murder me.†

J. KETCH. Come, directly.

PUNCH. I can't; I got one bone in my leg.

J. KETCH. And you've got one bone in your neck, but that shall be soon broken.—Then I must fetch you. (*he goes to the prison, and after a struggle, in which* PUNCH *calls out,* "Mercy! mercy! I'll never do so again!" JACK KETCH *brings him out to the front of the stage*)

PUNCH. Oh dear! Oh dear! Be quiet—can't you let me be?

J. KETCH. Now, Mr. Punch, no more delay. Put your head through this loop.

PUNCH. Through there! What for?

J. KETCH. Aye, through there.

Tassoni's "Secchia Rapita," Venice, 1747, to Orazio Toscanella,) with some lines quite in the spirit in which our hero speaks in the text.

"Non so più bello star, ch'entro d'un muro, &c.

A prison, truly, is a charming place,
    Where all the livelong day we may be idle ;
A blest retreat where mind has double space,
    Because our bodies we are forc'd to bridle :
Where all that we require is *given*, not *bought*,
    I mean all good things, and are but denied ill.
When to this happy rest we once are brought,
    It verifies the words of Aristotle—
Gross sense decays, and we have time for thought.

* A direct plagiarism from Shakspeare: "Master Barnardine, you must rise and be hanged." *Measure for Measure.*

† An instance how Punch's self-possession never forsakes him. In a single sentence he confutes all who contend that man by law should have power over the life of his fellow man.

PUNCH. What for?—I don't know how.

J. KETCH. It is very easy : only put your head through here.

PUNCH. What, so ? (*poking his head on one side of the noose*)

J. KETCH. No, no, here !

PUNCH. So, then ? (*poking his head on the other side*)

J. KETCH. Not so, you fool.

PUNCH. Mind who you call fool : try if you can do it yourself.   Only shew me how, and I do it directly.

J. KETCH. Very well; I will.   There, you see my head, and you see this loop : put it in, so. (*putting his head through the noose*)

PUNCH. And pull it tight, so ! (*he pulls the body forcibly down, and hangs* JACK KETCH) Huzza ! Huzza ! (PUNCH *takes down the corpse, and places it in the coffin: he then stands back*)

Enter two MEN, *who remove the gibbet, and placing the coffin upon it, dance with it on their shoulders grotesquely, and exeunt.*

PUNCH. There they go.   They think they have got Mr. Punch safe enough. (*sings*)

> They're out ! they're out ! I've done the trick !
> Jack Ketch is dead—I'm free ;
> I do not care, now, if Old Nick
> Himself should come for me.

> *Goes off and returns with a stick.   He dances about beating time on the front of the stage, and singing to the tune of "Green grow the rushes O."*

> > Right foll de riddle loll,
> > I'm the boy to do 'em all.
> > Here's a stick
> > To thump Old Nick,
> > If he by chance upon me call.

Enter the DEVIL.   *He just peeps in at the corner of the stage, and exit.*

PUNCH. (*much frightened, and retreating as far as he*

$$q^2$$

q^2

can) Oh, dear! Oh, lord! Talk of the devil, and he pops up his horns. There the old gentleman is, sure enough. (*a pause and dead silence, while* PUNCH *continues to gaze at the spot where the* DEVIL *appeared. The* DEVIL *comes forward)* Good, kind Mr. Devil, I never did you any harm, but all the good in my power.—There, don't come any nearer. How you do, Sir? *(collecting courage)* I hope you and all your respectable family well? Much obliged for this visit—Good morning—should be sorry to keep you, for I know you have a great deal of business when you come to London. (*the* DEVIL *advances*) Oh, dear! What will become of me? (*the* DEVIL *darts at* PUNCH, *who escapes, and aims a blow at his enemy: the* DEVIL *eludes it, as well as many others, laying his head on the platform, and slipping it rapidly backwards and forwards, so that* PUNCH, *instead of striking him, only repeatedly hits the boards)*   *Exit* DEVIL.

PUNCH. He, he, he! (*laughing*) He's off: he knew which side his bread buttered on. He one deep, cunning devil. (PUNCH *is alarmed by hearing a strange supernatural whirring noise, something like the rapid motion of fifty spinning wheels, and again retreats to the corner, fearfully waiting the event)*

Re-enter the DEVIL, *with a stick. He makes up to* PUNCH, *who retreats round the back of the stage, and they stand eyeing one another and fencing at opposite sides. At last the* DEVIL *makes a blow at* PUNCH, *which tells on the back of his head.*

PUNCH. Oh, my head! What is that for? Pray, Mr. Devil, let us be friends. *(the* DEVIL *hits him again, and* PUNCH *begins to take it in dudgeon, and to grow angry)* Why, you must be one very stupid Devil not to know your best friend when you see him. (*the* DEVIL *hits him again*) Be quiet, I say, you hurt me!—Well if you won't, we must try which is the best man,—Punch or the Devil.

(*here commences a terrific combat between the* DEVIL *and* PUNCH : *in the beginning, the latter has much the worst of it, being hit by his black adversary when and where he pleases ; at last, the*

DEVIL *seems to grow weary, and* PUNCH *succeeds in planting several heavy blows. The balance being restored, the fight is kept up for some time, and towards the* conclusion PUNCH *has the decided advantage, and drives his enemy before him. The* DEVIL *is stunned by repeated blows on the head and horns, and falls forward on the platform, where* PUNCH *completes his victory, and knocks the breath out of his body.* PUNCH *then puts his staff up the* DEVIL'S *black clothes, and whirls him round in the air, exclaiming,* " Huzza ! huzza ! the Devil's dead !"

Curtain.

CPSIA information can be obtained
at www.ICGtesting.com
Printed in the USA
LVOW04s1414160816
500614LV00044B/638/P